MX 99

CW01090895

The Third Reich Between Vision and Reality

German Historical Perspective Series
General Editors:
Gerhard A. Ritter and Anthony J. Nicholls

German Historical Perspectives/XII

The Third Reich Between Vision and Reality

New Perspectives on German History 1918–1945

Edited by
HANS MOMMSEN

Oxford • *New York*

First published in 2001 by
Berg
Editorial offices:
150 Cowley Road, Oxford, OX4 1JJ, UK
838 Broadway, Third Floor, New York, NY 10003-4812, USA

Berg is the imprint of Oxford International Publishers Ltd.

Library of Congress Cataloging-in-Publication Data

A catalogue record for this book is available from the Library of Congress.

British Library Cataloguing-in-Publication Data

A catalogue record for this book is available from the British Library

ISBN 1 85973 254 2 (Cloth)

Typeset by JS Typesetting, Wellingborough, Northants.
Printed in the United Kingdom by Antony Rowe Ltd, Chippenham, Wilts.

Contents

Editorial Preface

The purpose of this series of books is to present the results of research by German historians and social scientists to readers in English-speaking countries. Each of the volumes has a particular theme that will be handled from different points of view by specialists. The series is not limited to the problems of Germany but will also involve publications dealing with the history of other countries, with the general problems of political, economic, social and intellectual history as well as international relations and studies in comparative history.

We hope the series will help to overcome the language barrier that experience has shown obstructs the rapid appreciation of German research in English-speaking countries.

The publication of the series is closely associated with the German Visiting Fellowship at St Antony's College, Oxford, which has existed since 1965, having been originally funded by the Volkswagen Stiftung, later by the British Leverhulme Trust, by the Ministry of Education and Science in the Federal Republic of Germany, and starting in 1990, by the Stifterverband für die Deutsche Wissenschaft with special funding from C. & A. Mode Düsseldorf. Each volume is based on a series of seminars held in Oxford, which has been conceived and directed by the Visiting Fellow and organized in collaboration with St Antony's College.

The editors wish to thank the Stifterverband für die Deutsche Wissenschaft for meeting the expenses of the original lecture series and for generous assistance with the publication. They hope that this enterprise will help to overcome national introspection and to further international academic discourse and co-operation.

Gerhard A. Ritter   Anthony J. Nicholls

HANS MOMMSEN

Introduction

This collection of scholarly contributions on German history during the inter-war period focuses on the elements of continuity between the Weimar period and the National Socialist dictatorship, but tries simultaneously to shed light on several of the most controversial issues of recent research, especially the preconditions for the implementation of the Holocaust as well as the relative modernity and economic efficiency of the Nazi regime.

From different angles, the contributions to this volume coincide in their endeavour to analyse the ideological and psychological preconditions for Hitler's rise to power and the considerable popular support for his rule, which lasted well into the war. In many respects National Socialism skilfully exploited the resentment, particularly among the German upper and middle classes, arising from the defeat of 1918, which many were unwilling to accept. This must be perceived within the larger context of the political and intellectual crisis in Germany; as a reflection of social cleavages which had been considerably sharpened by the material losses of the war and the economic crises of the post-war period.

In dealing with the widespread acceptance of the use of violence in the political arena Bernd Weisbrod describes the vunerability above all of the German intellectuals and middle class to a fundamentalist appeal to the 'imagined community' of the nation and of an adoration of violence and sacrifice which then was utilized by Hitler and culminated in anti-Jewish persecution.

Parallel to this, Brigitte Hamann in her report on Hitler's formative years in Vienna shows convincingly that the future dictator was exposed to eccentric world views of a *völkisch* and racist persuasion in the Habsburg capital and acquired there a specifically visionary perception of politics. However, the extremely destructive influence of *völkisch* and nationalistic advisers during his stay in the Reichswehr group command IV in Munich early in 1919 have been crucial for the formation of his *Weltanschauung*.

In the following chapter Wolfgang Schieder depicts the impact the Fascist experiment in Italy had on the German bourgeois right which was ready to support any kind of leadership cult and perceived Mussolini's dictatorship as a model for the solution of Germany's domestic crisis. Schieder describes the deep impression Mussolini made on his German visitors, whom he would most frequently address in their mother tongue, and the early contact between leading members in the Fascist and Nazi parties. Moreover, he underlines the tactical use by Hitler of the widespread philo-fascism among the German elite and raises the question to what extent the sympathies of the German conservative elite with Italian Fascism paved the way for Hitler's seizure of power.

Turning to conditions under the Nazi dictatorship, Norbert Frei analyses the impact of the *Volkgemeinschaft* myth on the German population at large and its role in compensating for any clear-cut domestic political programme by presenting Germans with the visionary political goal of a classless society, excluding however all alien racial groups. He stresses the fact that the German population was strongly committed to the idea of the *Volkgemeinschaft* and that this contributed to the massive popularity of Hitler, especially after the victories over Poland and France. Its integretative function even withstood the burdens connected with the protracted war against the Soviet Union and did not wither away before the defeat at Stalingrad early in 1943, but turned then into a prevailing mood of emptiness and resignation. This created apathy, combined with an increasing, if unadmitted, feeling of complicity in Nazi crimes.

In contradiction to the widespread assumption that the NS regime successfully exploited the German economy for its ends and achieved an impressive economic expansion, Christoph Buchheim in his essay portrays Nazi economic policy as anything but a success story and argues that it inevitably led to complete economic disarray, although the latter was retarded by the ruthless economic exploitation of occupied countries. Thus he describes the uncoordinated and contradictory traits of the Nazi economic system, which had to rely upon unremitting expansion and escalating violence and was not able to achieve any long-term stability.

There existed, however, remarkable pockets of rationality, as Ulrich Herbert, by drawing a line from the *völkisch* anti-Semitic indoctrination practised in Weimar Republic universities to the rather consistent ideological world view of the leading officers in the Main Security Office, points out. In his view, the unremitting energy which led to the implementation of the 'Final Solution' emerged mainly from ideological premises and cannot be described simply as the outcome of bureaucratic processes. He argues, however, that, while the different varieties of anti-Semitic beliefs within the German population were a precondition for the Holocaust, its actual implementation relied on a progressive interaction between the local perpetrators and the central authorities of the SS, who were characterized by a calculating and unemotional anti-Jewish mentality.

In a concluding essay Hans Mommsen deals with the progressive dissolution of the Nazi regime, describing its ultimate decay after the battle of Stalingrad in January 1943 until its complete breakdown in May 1945. This chapter starts from the assumption that the Nazi regime in its decline exposed its very nature in a rather condensed form and returned to the concepts of the combat period before 1933 as well as to the revolutionary objectives which had been postponed in 1933/4. It took refuge in the dream of complete racial and political homogeneity to achieve either survival or a heroic downfall which would preserve the National Socialist ideal for future generations.

The recourse to unrestricted party rule and an overall mobilisation of the party for the war effort meant that there was no possibility of stopping a war that was already lost before the complete collapse occurred together with Hitler's suicide, which necessarily led to an all-embracing destruction of the Nazi state. The tendency of the Nazi movement to return to its origins revealed what all the time had been the key of the Nazi credo – the demand for unshakeable belief as an end in itself, which fitted well enough into the fundamentalist subcurrent in German political culture depicted by Bernd Weisbrod.

The collection of essays in this volume cannot include all the aspects of recent research on Germany in the inter-war period, but provides a representative picture of new trends and frames of reference within German historiography, designed to put the history of Nazi Germany into a broader social and intellectual context as well as overcoming the oversimplified interpretations presented by the theory of totalitarianism.

BERND WEISBROD

Violence and Sacrifice: Imagining the Nation in Weimar Germany

For some years now there has been talk about the alleged modernity of the Third Reich, its ugly modern face of barbarism as well as its hidden impact on the push towards modernity in post-war Germany. Some have read back the experience of the 1950s into the 'good years' of the Third Reich – or rather the myth of the *Wirtschaftswunder*, which was itself generated to forget the hardship experienced by refugees, the old and the unskilled. Some mistook what was 'modern' in National Socialist 'social policies' on the shop floor or in mass culture as a harbinger of 'modern times', when in fact it was merely a postscript to the mode of rationalization of the 1920s and the Weimar 'cult of modernity'. But this itself was very much a big city illusion which left the heartland of Germany untouched.[1]

This heartland was not only the neglected hinterland of the German provinces where the Protestant protagonists of the home town tradition first rallied to the Nazi cause.[2] *Der Aufstand der Provinz* was effective in its anti-modernist thrust, but it also fed on another hinterland of the German imagination which was at the heart of its mental map after the First World War: The German mind was obsessed with the trauma of the Great War. Hitler was, after all, 'undeniably the creation of his time, a creature of German imagination rather than, strictly speaking, of any social and economic forces.'[3] This is not, as might be conceived, a question of his *Weltanschauung*, consistent or otherwise, nor is it a question of a distinctive 'national project', which united all 'ordinary Germans'.[4] But the public impact of Goldhagen's book may remind us that we have shied away,

5

maybe for too long, from looking into that heartland of the German imagination, which was, ever since the Wars of Liberation of 1813, and especially so since the traumatic defeat in the Great War, haunted by the fear of failed nationhood.

The violent experience of war and its aftermath – the 'Myth of the War Experience' as George Mosse has it in capital letters[5] – was instrumental in reworking that 'redemptive nationalism' which the National Socialists preached to almost everybody outside the core of the Weimar faithful. They blended the cult of their martyrs with the cult of the war dead. The 'political soldier' of the Storm Troops in effect enacted the 'apotheosis of the fallen soldier': his youth was purified, his pledge redeemed, his death sanctified by the use of violence as national propaganda. The Nazi 'Kult um die toten Helden' invoked the war dead from their graves to help with the coming of the holy Reich.[6] This is not, of course, to argue that wartime nationalism was in itself some sort of self-explanatory driving force, neither during the war effort nor afterwards, but it may be seen as a pervasive, if less than tangible, collective state of mind in the hour of defeat.[7]

There is, however, an underlying assumption about the reworking of that 'Myth' in the radical nationalism of the Nazis – which is that the German public at large might have been impressed, but that the bourgeois elite somehow cynically mistook these ideas for mere propaganda. Even the most extreme behaviour and clearly unacceptable political aims seem to have been taken more or less for granted as forgivable tactics or at best a cunning ruse in the otherwise totally acceptable mission to unite the nation and rid it from the enemy within. Yet, as Norbert Elias has pointed out, the self-representation of the Nazis was not only the expression of their own belief system; their appeal was such that even the educated elites eventually fell prey to the kind of moral 'regression' which made them feel part of that promised land, the *Volksgemeinschaft*.[8]

Political violence played a central role in this process of regression, as can be shown on two levels: on the functional level of political violence in the breakup of the Weimar Republic, and on the affective level of myth-making through violence and sacrifice. According to Norbert Elias, the political appeal of violence in the challenge to the state monopoly of power in Weimar Germany goes a long way to explain the strange double-bind which projected the moral indifference of brutalized post-war politics well into the Third Reich.[9] But there is also the possibility that the moral impact of this phenomenon helped the respectable middle class to respond to Hitler's own quasi-religious *Opfersyndrom* without necessarily taking on board any of his mangled ideas.[10] It is here, not in any consistent *Weltanschauung*, that we need to look for the counterpart of Nazi propaganda in the German mind. Traces of it might be detected in a close reading of the first and foremost representative of the German 'Myth of the War Experience', Ernst Jünger. In his writings we find that his obsession with violence and sacrifice tapped into a strong undercurrent of almost religious political fervour which may help to explain the cross-class, cross-party and eventually even cross-cultural rally to the swastika.[11]

I

We know that the Nazis used very modern methods of electioneering, that they spoke in many tongues and promised almost anything to everybody, real socialism to the German worker, free credit and tariffs to the small entrepreneurs and farmers, a strong military state to the army, the destruction of Marxism to big business, a measure of 'reprofessionalization' to apolitical academics all round, and so on.[12] But above all they promised struggle, the struggle for survival not only as a nation, but also as a viable assertion of the individual's position in society, which one held, they claimed, on trust from the eternal *Volk*. This reading of the *Volksgemeinschaft* as *Kampfgemeinschaft* (People's Community as Fighting Community) was underscored by the relentless use and display of violence in campaigns. Despite some obvious misgivings about street brawling, even this seemed to pay electoral dividends, at least until the summer of 1932, and maybe even during the cleaning-up operations of 1933 and 1934.[13]

Why this political culture of violence should have struck a chord with bourgeois society at large is not easy to explain.[14] The Nazi activists were, after all, the kind of 'political soldiers' whose principles could not exactly be reconciled with the established value system of bourgeois behaviour. Their decidedly youthful and activist stance clearly set them apart from established forms of political life. As we know from Peter Merkl's work on the Abel collection of old fighters' life histories, their readiness to fight was fuelled by an intense hatred of bourgeois respectability, a deliberate drive for self-victimization and a desperate longing for male bonding in the comradeship of the *Männerbund*.[15] This proved some sort of substitute for the loss of family and career in the turmoil of bourgeois society during the 'Great Disorder' of war, revolution and inflation. But the tangible advantages of a mock-military career aside, the stormtroopers seem to have been driven by an almost irrational 'courage for fear' and 'longing for the test of life': 'Mut zur Angst', in Heidegger's philosophical shorthand, and 'Treue zum Tod' (loyalty to death) for their Führer, as in the Nibelungen. This was the creed of their 'active nihilism' which tapped into the sources of a broad stream of apocalyptic visions in German history.[16]

This paradox was also at the heart of Hitler's own gamble for power which – despite all his declarations of legality – played openly on the ambivalent attitude to violence not only among his volatile followers but also in society at large: As August Thalheimer had already observed in 1930, his Bonapartist promise of 'law and order' required the constant threat of violence, which the Nazi fighters were only too ready to provide, posing as Germany's shock troops of salvation.[17] As long as they tracked down communists in their territory, as long as they avoided confronting the police while publicly pretending to be doing their real job, they effectively undermined state authority and made themselves indispensable for onlookers with a cause: the 'new men' for the new state to come – with a bourgeois appeal to proletarian virility.[18]

The Nazi appeal to violence, therefore, rested on both, 'roughness and respectability', as Richard Bessel has shown.[19] But why is it that their skirmishes into red territory – their assumed role as private police – attracted so little opposition from the public at large? Why was it that this show of violence for violence's sake, this professed 'myth' of violence of Sorelian proportions, did not backfire politically but, as far as we can see, actually won votes? It is true that the SPD interior ministers made this threat of violence a cornerstone of their legal strategy for prosecuting Nazi organizations under the *Republik-schutzgesetz* already in 1930. But they found little support from the Reich authorities and the public at large to which this show of violence was deliberately addressed – until it was too late.[20] Part of the answer certainly lies in the self-proclaimed military potential supposedly available in the Nazi SA, which was regarded as a welcome reserve capacity in planning the rearmament of the Reichswehr. There was also the display of physical force by communists in defence of their territory: They not only hit back and beat the fascists, whoever they were deemed to be at the time, but they even attacked the police in acts of sheer terrorism, until this disastrous and uncontrollable policy shift was called off by the Communist Central Committee at the end of 1931.[21]

But this still does not explain why the Nazi story of self-victimization was generally accepted in the studiously one-sided reports of the bourgeois press on acts of violence and why even the nastier aspects of this new combative political style were treated sympathetically. As Friedrich Meinecke observed right after the September election of 1930, there was an uneasy relationship between the *Bürgertum* and the Nazis. They may be scorned for their economic demands and their rowdy street behaviour, he observed, but at the same time there was this constant belief in their future usefulness and reliability. In short, they were not just regarded as potentially politically useful, they were held – by degrees – in awe and admiration, just if they were playing from a hidden script which for some reason or other was denied to respectable society.[22]

And this they did, it would seem, because their virile behaviour provided the public with an oblique reminder of the war experience, now heightened by the excitement of the revolutionary threat. It played openly on the vigilante spirit of the bourgeois revolutionary experience, which, as Hans-Joachim Bieber has shown, was replete with more or less violent forms of self-protection.[23] Many of the Nazi old guard did have a bloody Freikorps background, but hundreds and thousands of bourgeois youths who had failed to be tested in the trenches also had a short spell under arms. They had rallied in numbers to that first 'bürgerliche Sammlungsbewegung' of the Weimar Republic, in which voluntary military units and civil guards had acted as a backup for the Freikorps who were taking their revenge in Munich, Berlin or the Ruhr. The Bolshevik scare was certainly over by 1923, but the show of physical force by Nazi activists played successfully on that counter-revolutionary vigilante spirit by simply pretending that Marxism had won the peace after all. Their violence, in substance and in form, was the symbolic replay of that post-war vigilantism by which the good citizens seemed to have been spared a real civil war for the time being, and which had lingered on as a substitute form of self-protection ever since the inflation.[24]

These arguments are, of course, far from the usual history of party politics, and proof is hard to come by. But it is evident that political violence was deeply ingrained in the structure of Weimar politics, with devastating effects during the final crisis of the republic. There were efforts at conscious manipulation on either side: Schleicher's alarmist claims in 1932 that the army could not cope with fighting both communists and Nazis ('Planspiel Ott') helped the demise of the presidential government by deliberately playing up the revolutionary scenario; the *Boxheim Documents* showed a desperate desire on the part of the Nazis for a revolutionary pretext for their Bartholomew's night. It also has to be said that the symbolic militarization of party politics was certainly not restricted to the NSDAP. The Reichsbanner did show up in strength for the parties of the Weimar Coalition, even if it and the more combative Iron Front were hardly prepared to fight. And on the Right the massive organization of the Stahlhelm was mobilizing the Protestant provinces in a military-style dress-rehearsal for fascism.[25]

But quite apart from revolutionary role playing and party show tactics there was another dimension to the appeal of Nazi violence in bourgeois society. Even among liberal democrats and democratic conservatives we find that strange attraction to the enigmatic figure of the young fighter which echoed the specifically masculine ideal of the German youth movement and the wartime mythmaking of Langemarck. The fascination for the fighting youth was professed over and over again in public declarations for the war dead and monumentalized in the memorial culture which sprang up in war cemeteries, school halls and public places everywhere.[26] But it was not only presented in the traditional code of Christian resurrection, it also showed up in private circles of the 'secret Germany' in the revivalist code of a redemptive *Jugendbewegung* imbued with a kind of *völkisch* exoticism. To take but one example, even a man like Willy Helpach, the presidential candidate of the Democrats in 1925 eventually found a strange delight in the primitive, uncivilized traits of the Nazi movement. It promised a shared virility and allowed for a *Volksgemeinschaft* of the senses, which seemed to establish male values in politics across the boundaries of party and even class.[27] But how virility could be mistaken for politics is quite another matter.

In terms of propaganda, however, there were limits to what violence could do. It is clear from the havoc caused by Hitler's wholehearted support for the Potempa murders in August 1932 that there was a limit to this tacit approval of political violence.[28] Pushing the desperate Weimar Republic over the edge with the welcome help of an unpleasant street gang was one thing, handing over the intellectual and spiritual leadership in that enterprise was quite another. Goebbels might have been correct in his diagnosis that there was a danger of exhaustion in permanent election victories.[29] The eruption of almost uncontrollable SA violence, especially in the East in the summer of 1932, gives a clear indication of the deep-seated frustration among the fighters who had counted on set dates and plans for the system to be toppled, by physical force if necessary. Now, they found themselves reined in again for another useless election which showed that the tide was running against them for the first time. They were neither indispensable nor was Hitler invincible, and this was a shattering experience for those who believed in his 'touch'.[30]

It is, however, open to dispute whether the slump in the Nazi vote in November 1932 was an indication of the heightened alarm of the bourgeois vote in the face of ever more radical Nazi tactics in strike and street actions against the Papen government or whether the almost chiliastic expectations projected on the Hitler-movement had simply run their course after he had spurned Hindenburg's call for power-sharing in August 1932. In the propaganda departments of the party it was simply assumed that the *Spießbürger*-vote had defected as the going was getting tougher.[31] The 'law and order' question had indeed acquired a new dimension with Papen's takeover of the Prussian Ministry of Interior and the police force from the Social Democrats. But on the whole, those close to Papen, like Edgar Julius Jung, who had himself revolted against 'Die Herrschaft der Minderwertigen' by firing a pistol at separatists in his young days, were still trapped in their belief of the future usefulness of the Nazis. They liked to see them as just the 'department for mass mobilization' in that great movement for national regeneration which they still hoped to control. It was only after the threatening escalation of a 'second revolution' that Jung warned, in Papen's famous Marburg speech of 17 June, 1934, against their 'adulation of violence which mistook brutality for vitality' – a warning for which he himself had to pay with his life a few days later in the so-called Röhm-Putsch.[32]

Whatever the chances of winning an outright victory by sheer intimidation, by 1933 the Nazi uses of violence and their tacit acceptance by a wide spectrum of the electorate and the political elite had established a political culture of violence which singled out the Marxist 'enemy within' as its prime target. Violence had certainly battered the defences of the socialist milieux in their urban strongholds.[33] This escalation of violence had simulated a quasi-revolutionary situation by challenging the state monopoly of power, and it eventually helped to ease the way for the terroristic cleansing operations of 1933 and 1934. As far as the Left was concerned, this could be seen as a promise well kept. Miracles could be worked. But, ironically, it was the direct involvement of the Führer himself in the murder of the SA leaders which firmly established the myth of Hitler the Saviour. Most of the police reports agree that eliminating the violent threat posed by still unsatisfied stormtroopers, even at the price of cold-blooded murder, met with a considerable degree of public approval, if not 'actual relief', as Goebbels claimed. This sentiment was even to be found among ex-Social Democrats or Communists who might have been tempted to believe in some sort of vindicative justice.[34]

Some time ago Detlev Peukert argued that these sentiments should be seen as a first measure of the 'emotional approval' ('affektive Zustimmung') of acts of state terrorism to come.[35] Hitler indeed announced in this context his intention relentlessly to exterminate all 'antisocial and sickly elements'. But in this matter, as well as with regard to the physical assault on the Jews in the *Reichskristallnacht* he was later forced to tread much more carefully. This might, therefore, be taking the argument too far. In general, however, Norbert Elias's analysis seems well founded. The deliberate erosion of the 'state monopoly of power' in Weimar's political culture of violence was a prerequisite for that 'disintegration of conscience' which, together with the experience of mass destruction in modern war, explains the high degree of moral indifference towards the elimination and extinction of the European Jews. But that is quite a different story.[36]

II

The plausibility of the above argument rests, however, on some tacit assumptions which need further clarification. There is still a missing link which would give credence to the assumption that there is more in the appeal of violence than just political convenience or the self-propelled dynamics of a crumbling political system. If there was an unadmitted attraction of violence not just for perpetrators but also for onlookers we have to assume an emotional premium on violence. Political violence played on the peculiarity of the German imagination which was reborn in war as a new national religion. This was indeed 'new' in the 'new nationalism' of the Weimar Republic, although it has to be said in Germany that nationalism has always been sanctified as a political religion by war, ever since the Wars of Liberation.[37] But violent self-sacrifice as a way to national redemption – this laboured idiom lent itself to a new religiosity in politics, after the 'nationalization of death' had reached its pinnacle in the Great War.

This mythical contamination of nationalism with violence has been somewhat overlooked in the recent debate on the quasi-religious quality of National Socialism. It is less a question of a coherent *Weltanschauung* or the liturgical evidence for a functioning Nazi church in the Third Reich, and more a case of the evangelical nature of redemptive nationalism which fuelled the Nazi claim for power through violence.[38] This fundamentalist stance harked back to that distinctive idolatry of nationhood which believed in its own immortality through self-sacrifice and which strove to achieve ultimate knowledge of national identity by eliminating the 'enemy within'.[39] In other words: Nazi 'violence as propaganda' not only evoked the bourgeois experience of anti-revolutionary vigilantism, it also negotiated a line of inclusion and exclusion, which went beyond questions of democratic rule or compromise and aimed straight at the mythical quality of pure nationhood by sacrifice. This vision established a sense of urgency, not so much as a code of conduct for everybody but as a way of imagining the fate of the nation.[40]

This also fell in line with the groundswell of political metaphysics, which in Carl Schmitt's influential writings heralded the ability to define – and eventually to kill – an enemy as the only true test of politics. Clearly parliamentary procedures failed this test – and not only in the eyes of the Nazis. The show of violence also reflected the leitmotiv of literary heroism, which reinvented wartime experience as an angst-ridden fulfilment of manliness, as in Ernst Jünger's *Battle as Inner Experience* (1922). They hailed each other as 'decisionists', who just like Heidegger, accepted the 'thrownness' – *die Geworfenheit* – as necessary for that intensity of feeling which mistook decisiveness for a decision, exertion for responsibility and the state for the will of the people.[41] They were all believers of a new creed, addicts of the ideology of 'must', as philosophers, political theorists or literary heroes. Ernst Jünger hailed Carl Schmitt's *Begriff des Politischen* enthusiastically as a landmine which would eventually blow up the helpless twaddle of European politics by its sheer cold-bloodedness and viciousness – never mind the political argument.[42] And it was Carl Schmitt himself who detected in Georges Sorel's 'myth', which was after all a 'myth of violence', the sacred force which would remythify the state.[43]

The intellectual lineages of this new belief-system are manifold and intricately interwoven, but in much of the Conservative Revolution this is the only common denominator in a whole range of otherwise contradictory strands of thought. The myth-hunger of its protagonists united their nationalist longing into a new and urgent kind of 'political religion' – albeit with an inherent tendency to deify the state, while National Socialism depended on a revivalist mobilization to keep up its charismatic momentum.[44] These intellectual endeavours may, therefore, be used as a wild compass in the No Man's Land of the German post-war imagination. This is especially so in the case of Ernst Jünger, the protagonist of the nationalist dream of trenchocracy.[45] He was certainly not just, as he claims in his Second World War journal *Strahlungen*, the seismograph which should not be held responsible for the volcanic eruption it registers; in his praise of violence he was himself part of that volcanic mental map of the nationalist imagination and the self-serving neglect of this achievement in his later literary career only proves the point.[46]

Ernst Jünger's war experience was reworked in *The Storm of Steel* (1920) and in a number of subsequent books as the apotheosis of those singular men of steel, who had survived the bloodiest, wildest and most brutal of all wars in the trenches – just like himself – because in their blind rage they had been able to stand the final test of manhood in killing and in offering up their lives for a sacred cause. These 'princes of the trenches' – who never retreat and have no mercy, who revel in blood and seek death in ecstasy – were, of course, straight out of Nietzsche: the cause of the fight mattered nought, what mattered was the beauty of the fight – it sanctified the cause.[47]

This well-laboured idiom justified the nationalist revival which Jünger himself stood for in the second half of the 1920s. The Great War – 'der große rote Schlußstrich unter der bürgerlichen Zeit' – he believed had heralded in a new age, in which the sacrifice of these men called for a new order. They had died in order for Germany to survive: the closing line in *The Storm of Steel* in its earlier versions and it was reiterated in the cold-blooded rhetoric of his political journalism.[48] Jünger did not think 'war a lovely business', as one English reviewer scathingly commented on the English edition. On the contrary, his 'embattled style' which speaks heroically of courage and fear is full of cold contempt for those who did not 'follow' and full of orgiastic exaltations in the face of abstract cruelty: 'contempt, in brief, not for death, but for all life that is lived on any other than the existential level'.[49] His magical invulnerability returns in an idiom of 'deathlessness' which is devoid of compassion and anxiety for the price of human suffering. War was clearly not 'his scourge', to use a famous phrase from Siegfried Sassoon, it was his glory, the glory of man in battle, the glory of living dangerously – and it speaks of the self-adulation of the self-appointed hero-martyr.

This kind of hero-worship had little to do with Thomas Carlyle's romantic preaching of historical heroes which was also popularized in the Third Reich. For the historian of the Conservative Revolution it marked Jünger out as a 'Gesinnungsmilitarist' (militarist by conviction) (Hans-Peter Schwarz), for the literary pundit as a 'Gesinnungsästhet' (aesthetic by conviction) (Karl-Heinz Bohrer),[50] but his war books are really public confessions, manifestos of male fundamentalism, a fundamentalism with a political cutting edge.[51] He preached political manliness as a means of national redemption and thus added a new appeal to political violence. When Jünger spelled out his political creed in dozens of political articles in the late 1920s, this fundamentalism came across as the only valid guarantee for a national rebirth in a utopian state, which he had seen in the trenches, a social, authoritarian and military state for men hardened in battle and united in a communion of minds. When, as a short-time Stahlhlem-intellectual, he called on the national youth movement to close ranks in 1926, he needed no programme, no tactics, no discussions. It was enough to push to the limits the final decision, to be ready for the necessary sacrifice, to do what fate ordains: 'We want Germanness, and we want it with might', he proclaimed, and he promised it would come about all of a sudden just like the 'Führer' who would emerge from this timeless and supreme exertion.[52]

For Jünger, and probably for many of his wartime generation, it did not matter what this exertion was actually called in the different national camps – heroism, *völkisch* idealism or even anti-Semitism – as long as there was this unshakable belief that the life of the nation had to be taken as a matter of 'blood and fate'; victory was at hand. The Work on the Myth ('Die Arbeit am Mythos'), as Hans Blumenberg called it, would also solve the notorious 'Jewish Question', as Jünger explained in a remarkable article in the well-established *Süddeutsche Monatshefte*, 1930: to promote the 'German Being' ('deutsche Gestalt') would take the sting out of the assimilated Jew, who was the real danger; it would kill off even the most hidden germ in the bright sun of heroic Germanness, without any of the unpleasant and inefficient disinfection-methods of popular anti-Semitism. It would deprive the Jews of their last illusion, to live in Germany as Germans, and put them before their last alternative, in Germany either to be a Jew or not to exist ('in Deutschland Jude zu sein, oder nicht zu sein').[53]

III

Jünger is certainly a special case and his popularity is still a matter of contention. But he was by far the most outspoken convert to the new creed, the myth of violence which in his aesthetic mode of self-effacement spoke the language of sacrifice while positively condoning ruthlessness and manliness as a political strategy. His example also shows how easily the 'heroic realism' of trenchocracy could be transformed into the total mobilization of the warrior-worker for a dehumanized technocracy.[54] But this is merely to remind ourselves that there were strong undercurrents in the metaphysical landscape of Weimar's political culture that appeals to violence could touch well beyond their obvious tactical value in the Nazi drive for power. We have to consider the possibility that it was not only the Nazis themselves who were true believers in their political cause. They were obviously preaching to a broad church which was highly suscept-ible to the myth of national sacrifice as a sacrifice of individuality. After the Great War a growing part of this liturgy was sung in that quasi-religious tune of the 'dear purchase', which according to the title of J. P. Stern's posthumous work was a specifically German theme in modernism. It idolized the heroism of the last stand, it called on the supreme sacrifice for no other reason than the morality of extreme exertion – and it established a deep-rooted fundamentalist assump-tion about salvation through violence.[55]

We have come to accept that there was an almost evangelical experience at the core of the Hitler-myth, not just modern propaganda techniques. And we take it for granted that the cult of the fallen acquired totem (or kitsch) status for Nazi society. We also have a pretty clear picture of how Hitler (with his Austrian education and the help of Goebbels) got himself into the mood for the great mission as Saviour-Führer which turned history into prophecy.[56] But we still lack a convincing answer to the intriguing question as to how that longing for a communion of minds was already programmed into the nation. One part of the answer may lie in the effect of political violence on Weimar politics, not just in its function for the erosion of credible republicanism, but also in the mood and style of a politics of national urgency. The other side of the coin may show a high degree of susceptibility within the collective mind to a fundamentalist appeal for the embattled, not just 'imagined community' of the nation. This goes a long way to explain the appeal of political violence – over and above the counter-revolutionary vigilantism and outside the Nazi constituency as such. In both cases, Nazism as event, and Nazism as cult, violence played a vital role.

Notes

1. Hans Mommsen, 'Nationalsozialismus als vorgetäuschte Modernisierung', in id. (ed.), *Der Nationalsozialismus und die deutsche Gesellschaft. Ausgewählte Aufsätze*, Reinbek 1991, 405–27; (English in: *From Weimar to Auschwitz* (Princeton: Princeton University Press, 1991); Norbert Frei, 'Wie modern war der Nationalsozialismus?,' *Geschichte und Gesellschaft* 19 (1993) 367–87; Bernd Weisbrod, 'Der Schein der Modernität. Zur Historisierung der "Volksgemeinschaft"', in Karsten Rudolph and Christl Wickert (eds), *Geschichte als Möglichkeit. Über die Chancen der Demokratie, Festschrift Helga Grebing* (Essen: Klartext, 1995), 224–42.

2. Peter Fritzsche, *Rehearsals for Fascism. Populism and Political Mobilization in Weimar Germany* (Oxford: Oxford University Press, 1990).

3. Modris Eckstein, *Rites of Spring. The Great War and the Birth of the Modern Age* (New York: Anchor Books, 1990), 324.

4. For two completely different but basically flawed versions of this 'ideas-into-politics' approach cf. Frank Lothar Kroll, *Utopie als Ideologie: Geschichtsdenken und politisches Handeln im Dritten Reich* (Paderborn: Schöningh, 1998); and Daniel Goldhagen, *Hitler's Willing Executioners. Ordinary Germans and the Holocaust* (New York: Knopf, 1996), recently criticized not only for its arguments but also for its public effects in Johannes Heil and Rainer Erb (eds), *Geschichtswissenschaft und Öffentlichkeit. Der Streit um Daniel J. Goldhagen* (Frankfurt/M.: Fischer, 1998).

5. George L. Mosse, *Fallen Soldiers. Reshaping the Memories of the World Wars* (Oxford: Oxford University Press, 1990).

6. Sabine Behrenbeck, *Der Kult um die toten Helden: nationalsozialistische Mythen, Riten und Symbole; 1923 bis 1945* (Vierow bei Greifswald: SH-Verlag, 1996). Jay W. Baird, 'To Die for Germany. Heroes in the German Pantheon', Indiana 1990.

7. L. L. Farrar Jr., 'Nationalism in Wartime. Critiquing the Conventional Wisdom', in Frans Coetzee and Marylin Shevin-Coetzee (eds), *Authority, Identity and the Social History of the Great War* (Oxford: Berghahn Books, 1995), 133–51.

8. For a subtle reading of the behavioural standards of the German middle classes and their political 'regression' in the Nazi belief-system see Norbert Elias, 'Der Zusammenbruch der Zivilisation', in id., *Studien über die Deutschen. Machtkämpfe und Habitusentwicklung im 19. und 20. Jahrhundert* (Frankfurt/M.: Suhrkamp 1989), 391–516, especially 411.

9. This argument is outlined in Norbert Elias, 'Zivilisation und Gewalt. Über das Staatsmonopol der körperlichen Gewalt und seine Durchbrechung', in *Studien über die Deutschen*, 223–70 and 282–94.

10. For the religious connotations of Hitler's 'language of sacrifice' see J. P. Stern, *Hitler. The Führer and the People* (London: Fontana, 1975), ch. 3. In his monumental Hitler biography Ian Kershaw operates with

the Weberian concept of 'charisma': *Hitler. 1889–1936: Hubris* (London: Allen Lane, 1998); see also his comparative use of 'charismatic authority' in '"Working towards the Führer": reflections on the nature of the Hitler dictatorship', in Moshe Lewin (eds), *Stalinism and Nazism: Dictatorships in Comparison* (Cambridge: Cambridge University Press, 1997), 88–106.

11. The two lines of argument are first explored in: Bernd Weisbrod, 'Gewalt in der Politik. Zur politischen Kultur in Deutschland zwischen den beiden Weltkriegen', *Geschichte in Wissenschaft und Unterricht* 43 (1992), 391–404; and idem, 'Military Violence and Male Fundamentalism: Ernst Jünger's Contribution to the Conservative Revolution', in: *History Workshop Journal* (2000) 49, 69–94.

12. Cf. Thomas Childers (ed.), *The Formation of the Nazi Constituency 1919–1933* (London: Croom Helm, 1986).

13. Idem, Eugene Weiss, 'Voters and Violence: Political Violence and the Limits of National Socialist Mass Mobilization', *German Studies Review* 13 (1990), 481–98. For the approval of Nazi murders in the name of law and order see Mathilde Jamin, 'Das Ende der "Machtergreifung" und seine Wahrnehmung in der Bevölkerung', in Wolfgang Michalka (ed.), *Die nationalsozialistische Machtergreifung* (Paderborn: Ferdinand Schöningh, 1984), 207–19.

14. On the loss of security – in *Besitz, Bildung* and *Anstand* – cf. Bernd Weisbrod, 'The Crisis of Bourgeois Society in Interwar Germany', in Richard Bessel (ed.), *Fascist Italy and Nazi Germany. Comparisons and Contrasts* (Cambridge: Cambridge University Press, 1996), 23–39.

15. Cf. Peter H. Merkl, *The Making of a Stormtrooper* (Princeton: Princeton University Press, 1980). For the best analysis of the practical operations see Richard Bessel, *Political Violence and the Rise of Nazism. The Storm Troopers in Eastern Germany 1925–1934* (New Haven: Yale University Press, 1984).

16. For this apocalyptic dimension see Klaus Vondung, *Die Apokalypse in Deutschland* (München: Deutscher Taschenbuch Verlag, 1988).

17. August Thalheimer, 'Über den Faschismus', *Gegen den Strom. Organ der KPD* (Opposition) 3 (1930), reprinted in Wolfgang Abendroth (ed.), Otto Bauer, Herbert Marcuse, Arthur Rosenberg et al., *Faschismus und Kapitalismus. Theorien über die sozialen Ursprünge und die Funktion des Faschismus* (Frankfurt: Europäische Verlagsanstalt, 1967), 19–38.

18. Eve Rosenhaft, 'Links gleich rechts? Militante Straßengewalt um 1930', in Thomas Lindenberger and Alf Lüdtke (eds), *Physische Gewalt. Studien zur Geschichte der Neuzeit* (Frankfurt: Suhrkamp, 1995), 238–75.

19. Richard Bessel, 'Violence as Propaganda. The Role of the Storm Troopers in the Rise of National Socialism', in Childers (ed.), *Formation*, 131–46.

20. Eike Hennig, 'Politische Gewalt und Verfassungsschutz in der Endphase der Weimarer Republik', in: Rainer Eisfeld and Ingo Müller (eds), *Gegen*

die Barbarei. Essays Robert M. W. Kempner zu Ehren (Frankfurt: Athenäum, 1989), 107–30. See also Wolfgang Pyta, *Gegen Hitler und für die Republik. Die Auseinandersetzung der deutschen Sozialdemokratie mit der NSDAP in der Weimarer Republik* (Düsseldorf: Droste, 1989).

21. Eve Rosenhaft, *Beating the Fascists? The German Communists and Political Violence 1929–1933* (Cambridge: Cambridge University Pres, 1983).

22. Cf. Friedrich Meinecke, *Nationalsozialismus und Bürgertum*, in *Politische Schriften und Reden. Gesammelte Werke*, vol. II (Darmstadt, 1955), 442 (first published in *Kölnische Zeitung*, no. 696, 21 Dec. 1930).

23. Hans-Joachim Bieber, *Bürgertum in der Revolution. Bürgerräte und Bürgerstreiks in Deutschland 1919–1920* (Hamburg: Christians, 1992).

24. On the real – not just imagined – threat of violent social protest in the Prussian province of Saxony see Dirk Schumann, 'Der aufgeschobene Bürgerkrieg. Sozialer Protest und Politische Gewalt in Deutschland 1923', *Zeitschrift für Geschichtswissenschaft* 6 (1996), 526–44; on the nexus of violence and the self-protection mentality triggered by the inflation see Martin H. Geyer, *Verkehrte Welten. Revolution, Inflation und Moderne: München 1914–1924* (Göttingen: Vandenhoeck & Ruprecht, 1998), 391ff.

25. Fritzsche, *Rehearsals*.

26. George L. Mosse, 'Soldatenfriedhöfe und nationale Wiedergeburt. Der Gefallenenkult in Deutschland', in Klaus Vondung (ed.), *Kriegserlebnis. Der Erste Weltkrieg in der literarischen Gestaltung und symbolischen Deutung der Nationen* (Göttingen: Vandenhoeck & Ruprecht, 1980), 241–61; idem, *Fallen Soldiers. Reshaping the Memory of the World Wars* (Oxford: Oxford University Press, 1990); see also Reinhard Koselleck and Michael Jeismann (eds), *Der politische Totenkult: Kriegerdenkmäler in der Moderne* (München: Fink, 1994), and Jay Winter (ed.), *Sites of Memory, Sites of Mourning* (Cambridge: Cambridge University Press, 1995).

27. For an example of this see Bernd Weisbrod, 'Das "Geheime Deutschland" und das "Geistige Bad Harzburg". Friedrich Glum und das Dilemma des demokratischen Konservativismus am Ende der Weimarer Republik', in Christian Jansen, Lutz Niethammer and Bernd Weisbrod (eds), *Von der Aufgabe der Freiheit. Politische Verantwortung und bürgerliche Gesellschaft im 19. und 20. Jahrhundert. Festschrift für Hans Mommsen zum 5. November 1995* (Berlin: Akademie, 1995), 285–308.

28. Thomas Childers, 'The Limits of National Socialist Mobilisation: The Elections of 6 November 1932 and the Fragmentation of the Nazi Constituency', in idem (ed.), *Formation*, 232–59.

29. Joseph Goebbels, *Vom Kaiserhof zur Reichskanzlei. Eine historische Darstellung in Tagebuchblättern* (München: Eher, 1934), 87.

30. Bessel, *Political Violence*.

31. Childers, 'Limits', 244; Goebbels, *Kaiserhof*, 191f.

32. See Klemens von Klemperer, *Germany's New Conservatism: Its History and Dilemma in the Twentieth Century* (Princeton: Princeton University Press, 1968), 210f.

33. On the local nature of these vicious attacks see Detlef Schmiechen-Ackermann, *Nationalsozialismus und Arbeitermilieu. Der nationalsozialistische Angriff auf die proletarischen Wohnquartiere und die Reaktion in den sozialistischen Vereinen* (Bonn: Dietz, 1998).

34. Jamin, 'Ende', 215. For this cornerstone of the 'Hitler myth' see also Ian Kershaw, *Hitler*, ch. XII.

35. Detlev Peukert, *Volksgenossen und Gemeinschaftsfremde. Anpassung, Ausmerze und Aufbegehren unter dem Nationalsozialismus* (Köln: Bund Verlag, 1982), 89.

36. For a subtle analysis of the effect of total war on the imagination of total extinction see Omer Bartov, 'The European Imagination in the Age of Total War', in idem (ed.), *Murder in our Midst. The Holocaust, Industrial Killing, and Representation* (Oxford: Oxford University Press, 1996), 33–50; and for the extension into instrumental anti-Semitism see idem 'Defining Enemies, Making Victims: Germans, Jews and the Holocaust', *The American Historical Review* 103 (1998), 771–816.

37. Dietmar Klenke, 'Nationalkriegerisches Gemeinschaftsideal als politische Religion. Zum Vereinsnationalismus der Sänger, Schützen und Turner am Vorabend der Einigungskriege', *Historische Zeitschrift* 260 (1995), 395–448.

38. See the debate in Hans Mommsen, 'Nationalsozialismus als politische Religion', in Hans Maier and Michael Schäfer (eds) *'Totalitarismus' und 'Politische Religionen'. Konzepte des Diktaturvergleichs*, Bd. II (Paderborn: Schöningh, 1996), 173–223; also Michael Ley and Julius H. Schoeps (eds), *Der Nationalsozialismus als politische Religion* (Bodenheim: Philo, 1997).

39. On the general argument see Peter Berghoff, *Der Tod des politischen Kollektivs. Politische Religion und das Sterben und Töten für Volk, Nation und Rasse* (Berlin: Akademie, 1997); also Dirk Richter, *Nation als Form* (Opladen: Westdeutscher Verlag, 1996).

40. For the Fascist counterpart see Emilio Gentile, *The Sacralization of Politics in Fascist Italy* (Cambridge, Mass.: Harvard University Press, 1996).

41. For an early assessment of the 'decisionist' triangle see Christian von Krockow, *Die Entscheidung. Eine Untersuchung über Ernst Jünger, Carl Schmitt, Martin Heidegger* (Stuttgart: Enke, 1958).

42. In a letter to Carl Schmitt, 14 Oct. 1930, in: Paul Noack, *Carl Schmitt. Eine Biographie* (Berlin: Propyläen, 1993), 108.

43. Carl Schmitt, *Die geistesgeschichtliche Lage des heutigen Parlamentarismus* (München: Duncker & Humblot, 1926), 77ff.

44. See Stefan Breuer, *Anatomie der Konservativen Revolution* (Darmstadt: Wissenschaftliche Buchgesellschaft, 1993), 194, who (unconvincingly) discards the whole concept of the 'Conservative Revolution' in favour of a diluted notion of 'New Nationalism'. For a politically rather naive reading of the technical illusion of the Conservative Revolution, without

any of its violent myth-making, see Rolf Peter Sieferle, *Die Konservative Revolution. Fünf biographische Skizzen* (Frankfurt: Fischer, 1995).

45. Two biographies have recently tried to integrate the vast literature on Jünger: Thomas Nevin, *Ernst Jünger and Germany. Into the Abyss 1914–1945* (London: Constable), 1997; and Paul Noack, *Ernst Jünger. Eine Biographie* (Berlin: Alexander Fest Verlag), 1998, both with very little tendency to confront the political impact of his aesthetic self-mystification. See also Hans-Harald Müller and Harro Segeberg (eds), *Ernst Jünger im 20. Jahrhundert* (München: Fink, 1995).

46. For more detail see Weisbrod, 'Military Violence'.

47. See Steven E. Aschheim, *The Nietzsche Legacy in Germany 1890–1990* (Berkeley: University of California Press, 1992), 158ff. and for Jünger's ideal worker for the total mobilization: ibid. 199f.

48. For his political journalism, still not reprinted as part of his oeuvre, see Bruno W. Reimann and Renate Haßel, *Ein Ernst-Jünger-Brevier. Jüngers politische Publizistik 1920 bis 1933. Analyse und Dokumentation* (Marburg: Verlag des Bundes demokratischer Wissenschaftler und Wissenschaftlerinnen, 1991); quote from 'Über die Gefahr', *Widerstand* 6 (1931), 67, in ibid. 79.

49. See J. P. Stern, *Ernst Jünger* (New Haven: Yale University Press, 1958), 58.

50. Hans-Peter Schwarz, *Der konservative Anarchist. Politik und Zeitkritik Ernst Jüngers* (Freiburg: Rombach, 1962); Karl-Heinz Bohrer, *Die Ästhetik des Schreckens. Die pessimistische Romantik und Ernst Jüngers Frühwerk* (München: Hanser, 1978).

51. This political dimension of masculinity is somewhat blurred in George L .Mosse, *The Image of Man: The Creation of Modern Masculinity* (New York: Oxford University Press, 1996).

52. 'Schließt Euch zusammen', in *Standarte. Wochenschrift des Neuen Nationalismus*, 3 June 1926, reprinted in Karl O. Paetel, *Versuchung oder Chance? Zur Geschichte des deutschen Nationalbolschewismus* (Göttingen: Musterschmidt, 1965), 56.

53. 'Über Nationalismus und Judenfrage', *Süddeutsche Monatshefte*, 27 Sept. 1930, 843–5. See also Jean-Luc Favier, 'Ernst Jünger et les Juifs', *Les Temps Modernes* 51, Aout–Sept. 1996, 102–30.

54. See the mystification of man as the ultimate weapon in his *Der Arbeiter* (1932).

55. J. P. Stern, *The Dear Purchase. A Theme in German Modernism* (Cambridge: Cambridge University Press, 1995), 183ff. (on Jünger).

56. Kershaw, *Hitler*, passim. On the lasting reflection of this attraction see Saul Friedländer, *Kitsch und Tod: der Widerschein des Nationalsozialismus*, revised edn. (Frankfurt: Fischer, 1999).

BRIGITTE HAMANN

Hitler and Vienna: The Truth about his Formative Years

The following chapter is based on extended study of the last years of the Austro-Hungarian Empire and its impact on the formation of Hitler's political visions and concepts that were to become crucial in his career as the German dictator.

Between the ages of 18 and 24 Hitler lived in Vienna from 1907 to 1913, a phase that could be called his post-adolescent period, when the political *Weltanschauung* is usually formed. The findings presented in my recently published book *Hitler's Vienna*[1] make it quite clear that the young Hitler was completely dependent on the stream of contemporary political and social ideas of a certain social and ethnic section of the population of Vienna at the time of the *fin-de-siècle*: the extreme nationalistic Germans of Austria, that is to say, those Germans who were anti-liberal and anti-Social Democratic. In studying the *Zeitgeist* of these circles it becomes strikingly clear that the ideas Hitler and the National Socialists were to propagate in the Weimar Republic were far from being original. To put it more briefly: the politician Hitler copied the ideas and political slogans he absorbed in Vienna.

At the same time, the political style and the visionary schemes which were symptomatic of right-wing agitation in late imperial Vienna left a lasting imprint on Hitler's understanding of society and state, and thus provided the foundation on which he would later build his concrete political work.

My study of Hitler's Vienna focuses on two aspects – on the one hand a picture of the Vienna which formed young Hitler's political, cultural, social and economic environment in the years between 1907 and 1913, and on the other a biography of the young Hitler until 1913 when he left Vienna for Munich.

One of the greatest obstacles to a treatment of these early years consists in the fact that reliable sources are extremely scarce, while a great many falsifications and errors have led even thorough scholars to draw completely misleading conclusions, especially where Hitler's early political views were concerned.

Hitler himself put a lot of energy into suppressing even the smallest details of his biography. For example: in 1938 the Nazis removed all registration forms of the young Hitler from the registration office in Vienna and passed them on to the NSDAP archive in Berlin. Nobody could access any information about where he had lived during his Vienna phase – and as a result of this nobody could ask his former landladies or his companions in the men's hostel for information about him.

Instead – since there were naturally many speculations about Hitler's life in Vienna, and journalists were keen to obtain stories of the Führer's youth there – the Nazis presented a certain house as 'the house the Führer lived during his youth as an unknown student'. This middle-class house in a better district of Vienna (the 9th district, Simon Denkgasse 9) was depicted in the newspapers and photographed by the tourists. Hitler youths were posted as guards in front of it. The door was decorated with a huge picture of the Führer. But Hitler never lived in that house. And the fact that he lived in a men's hostel for nearly four years remained unknown.

Hitler wished that no other sources for his early biography should emerge, apart from his own record in *Mein Kampf*. This account in *Mein Kampf* about his youth in Austria is very extensive,[2] as Hitler even uses his early years to present his political slogans and to turn them into 'the school of my life'. That concerns above all his stories about his hard times as a construction worker in Vienna who had been persecuted by the trade unions – false claims which suited Hitler's image as a worker, and which were quoted frequently even in scholarly studies.

However, there is no proof at all that Hitler worked in the construction industry, and it is symptomatic that no eyewitness has been found who met him there.

And none of his companions in the men's hostel mentioned that Hitler had ever done manual work. On the contrary, his companion Reinhold Hanisch stressed that the young Hitler was not even strong enough to shovel snow in the winter. In fact,[3] he was extremely lazy and inefficient even when compared with his fellows in the hostel. And he was so incompetent at earning his living that his very poor companions had to present him with clothes and bread. He would spend his days reading newspapers and cheap booklets, and he liked to deliver extended lectures to his colleagues during the evenings in the hostel. His rhetorical efforts were not much appreciated by them, and he became a figure of fun.

In order to achieve a modest living and to pay the rent in the men's hostel during the time after 1910, he would paint postcards for tourists, copied from photographs or drawings. Because he was too shy to sell his products himself, he depended on his colleagues to offer them to the public. At first Hanisch was enlisted, then he preferred others such as Josef Neumann or Siegfried Löffner.

Because of the lack of written sources about Hitler's Vienna years, we have to rely mainly on eyewitness reports from a later period. Unfortunately, almost every one of the historians of Hitler's early years failed to check their reliability. In addition, eyewitness reports usually mixed up true and invented information. An outstanding example of this is Reinhold Hanisch, who met Hitler when he was without shelter and gave him the idea of earning money by painting postcards. Hanisch wrote his memoirs in the early 1930s and has often been accused of not telling the truth. But to my surprise it turned out that names and dates mentioned by him prove to be correct – possibly because Konrad Heiden, Hitler's first biographer,[4] on whose initiative Hanisch wrote his memoirs, controlled him strictly. Yet Hanisch is not at all trustworthy when he refers to Hitler's paintings, in which Heiden took no special interest. Hanisch usually conceals the truth about this because in the 1930s he made his living by forging 'Hitler-paintings' for sale at high prices. Thus Hanisch gave himself a bogus authenticity.

Another case concerns the rather short record by Karl Honisch, another companion in the men's hostel.[5] Honisch had been ordered to write down his recollections by the NSDAP archive in 1938, and therefore felt compelled to say nothing but positive things about the early Hitler. The major part of his report is nothing more than a copy of a brochure dealing with the men's hostel, which had appeared in 1908 in Vienna. But Honisch is the only eyewitness who stated that Hitler did not go from Vienna to Munich alone but had a friend who went with him – a fact Hitler himself never mentioned; nor did – surely on Hitler's orders – the family Popp in Munich who let a room to the two men. I have been able to identify this friend as Rudolf Häusler. The two friends lived in one room together in Munich for months and were separated only in August 1914 when Häusler returned to Vienna to join the Austro–Hungarian army. Häusler lived in anonymity until his death in 1973 in Vienna. His daughter told me various details about the young Hitler which don't fit the self-image Hitler created in *Mein Kampf*.

A totally unreliable source is Josef Greiner, who claimed to belong to Hitler's friends in the men's hostel. His book, published in 1947, was the first publication on the subject to appear after the Second World War, containing a lot of sensational stories about Hitler's youth in Vienna.[6] Greiner was the primary source for the assumption that Hitler's anti-Semitism resulted from a sexual experience with a Jewish prostitute who allegedly infected him with syphilis – a claim easily disproved by the Wassermann test that was made of Hitler's blood in 1941. Another story by Greiner claims that Hitler had raped a young girl acting as his artistic model. But Hitler never did life studies and only painted architectural sites.

Greiner's sensational reports were highly estimated by biographers, not only because they lent colour to the otherwise tedious life story of the adolescent Hitler, but also because they fitted the common picture of Hitler as a criminal and violent individual, which they projected into his youth as well. But the young Hitler in Vienna was not yet a criminal and as far as his relations to women were concerned, he was extremely shy and totally inexperienced.

All this may show that the primary obstacle for a serious invest-igation of the formative years of Hitler consists in the continuous repetition of the information provided by his own accounts in *Mein Kampf* or by witnesses whose credibility nobody had checked.

The absence of primary sources covering the Vienna period suggested another research strategy to me, namely to research the events, social conditions and political climate surrounding him through his Vienna years. This context was of the greatest importance as it was definitely the Vienna years in which Hitler's perception of politics was formed. He never had direct contact with political activities and did not belong to any political party or organization. As a typical bystander, he remained a loner and learned only from observation. Hence, he was more interested in slogans and ideological concepts than in political actions.

For these reasons, I painted a picture of the political and social climate of contemporary Vienna, of the localities where Hitler lived, the districts and streets where he spent his days, the institutions, among them the parliament, which he visited. Moreover, I described the politicians whom he might have admired, the books and newspapers he used to read, and last but not least the national politics of the multinational state as well as the economy and the lifestyle of the pre-war period. The specific conditions of the multinational empire and its capital, which underwent an increasing process of deliberate Germanization during the period of Karl Lueger's tenure as mayor, form the context in which Hitler lived.

The confusion within the Austrian parliament and the perennial strife between competing nationalistic fractions after the introduction of the general suffrage, impressed Hitler, who frequently attended its sessions. Like other spectators he regarded it as a political curiosity and a public disgrace. The Reichsrat comprised at least ten different nationalities and languages, hampered by the absence of interpreters and continuous attempts at obstruction. These first experiences with the parliamentary system and its deficiencies left their imprint on Hitler's political imagination. Following his favourite political party, the Austrian 'Alldeutsche' (Pan-Germans) under the leadership of its German 'Führer' Georg von Schönerer, Hitler took the incompetence of the new 'democratic' parliament as proof that democracy would lead to political chaos and the ruin of the state. Like his political idol Schönerer and the newspapers of the Alldeutsche, he thought that only a suffrage which gave more rights and votes to the 'noble race' of the Germans could guarantee a secure political life. Therefore it would be necessary to withdraw equal rights from the non-German nationalities because of their 'natural' inferiority.

Vienna, seen through Hitlers's eyes, was not the famous *fin-de-siècle* Vienna of modern artists like Schiele and Kokoschka, writers like Schnitzler and Stefan Zweig, or scientists like Sigmund Freud. Neither was it the courteous Vienna full of anecdotes about the lovely Empress Elisabeth and the Emperor Francis Joseph, the leading aristocrats and their luxurious lifestyle. Hitler's Vienna has remained unknown. It was the Vienna of the poor, of the unemployed young men coming from the provinces to the capital, as Hitler came from Linz. It was the Vienna of the homeless and the jobless who did not participate in modern art and literature. They would even call this modern art 'jüdisch entartet' (degenerate Jewish) – a term that became increasingly popular.

In Vienna a lot of hatred was harboured against strangers and immigrants, as well as a lot of Germanic nationalism in the multinational capital. Social misery, a housing shortage and, last but not least, a vitriolic anti-semitism, existed in a city where nearly 10 per cent of the population adhered to the Jewish Faith – about 200,000 individuals. And there were some politicians who succeeded in confirming all the frustrations and anxieties of the poor. Four of them became important for the political world-view of the young Hitler: Schönerer, Lueger, Karl Hermann Wolf and Franz Stein.

Georg von Schönerer was the leader of the extremist German nationalist party in Austria, called the 'Alldeutsche'. In this movement we can find a great many of the ideological and propagandistic slogans later used by the Nazis. For example, whenever Schönerer appeared in public he was greeted by his admirers with the cry: 'Heil dem Führer' ('Salute the Leader'). The term 'Heil' was the greeting within the pan-German movement since about 1900. To be called the 'Führer' was an invention by Schönerer, who regarded himself as the leader of the Austrian Germans. His aim was 'Alldeutschland', the unification of all Germans in the German Reich under the dynasty of the Hohenzollerns. This implied the demolition of the multinational state of the Habsburgs, the 'Rassenbabylon', a term which later on Hitler also came to use. Whenever the Schönerer group gathered at their meetings in Vienna, there was a sign on the door 'No admittance for Jews' or 'For Aryans only'.

Schönerer called for a strict segregation of the Germans from all the other nations in Austria – Slavs, Romanians, Jews and others – in line with the slogan 'Durch Reinheit zur Einheit' ('Through purity towards unity').

It was Schönerer who popularized racial anti-Semitism in Austria and who demanded special laws to restrict the human rights of the Jews and to revoke the emancipation they had achieved in 1867. Their admission to state schools and to the universities should be permitted only in proportion to their numbers. Furthermore, he demanded their exclusion from public offices, from large trading companies and from public life.

Schönerer's political and nationalistic programme focused on the slogan that 'anti-Semitism was the greatest national achievement of the century'. Consequently, the pan-German associations and clubs excluded all Germans of Jewish descent. Thus, the infamous 'Arier-paragraph' came into being, according to which even assimilated Jews who felt themselves to be German, like Theodor Herzl or Sigmund Freund and many others, were also excluded. In the eyes of Schönerer and his followers, a human being of Jewish descent was not worthy of belonging to the German people and dwelling among them. Schönerer coined the extremely anti-Semitic slogan of the so-called 'Juden-knechte' (Jewish serfs), to denote all those Christians who maintained social ties with their Jewish neighbours and colleagues.

At the same time, Schönerer propagated the cult of Germanic traditions. His followers would give their children allegedly Germanic names such as Thusnelda, Friedegilde or Kriemhild, as the Nazis were also to do later on. In his hatred of the 'Roman' 'international' Catholic Church he propagated the 'German' Protestant church with the slogan 'Los von Rom'. He introduced a German calendar for use by 'real Germans', with German names for months counting not from the birth of Christ, but from the battle of Noreja in 113 BC, when the ancient Germans defeated the Romans for the first time. Schönerer's entourage discussed obscure philosophies and methods of how to cultivate and to breed a pure German race. They called for marriage laws according to which marriages between persons of German descent and persons of Slavic or Jewish origin should be prohibited in order to purify the German race from alien blood.

Hitler was confronted with all these elements of Viennese extremist anti-Semitism and their ideological components. It may be of interest in this context that Hitler in his first Vienna year lived in Stumpergasse, a few houses from the office of the small newspaper *Alldeutsches Tagblatt* which propagated all these views. We can be sure that the first newspaper the young Hitler read every morning was this one, which he could read in the window display.

Two other German nationalist politicians turned out to be especially important for the emerging political concepts of Hitler. The first was Karl Hermann Wolf, the leader of the German Radical Party. He became widely known for successfully disrupting parliamentary proceedings by violent methods. Wolf was the outstanding hero in the German–Czech street battles in Prague and in Vienna, and did not hesitate to advocate the use of violence in political strife.

Another model was Franz Stein, the leader of the German workers' party, which belonged to the Austrian pan-German movement. Stein was regarded as an embittered enemy of the allegedly 'Jewish' international Social Democrats. He fought a continuous struggle for withdrawing the German workers from the Social Democratic Party and including them in his German National Socialist party, in fact without success. Stein incidentally imitated the Czech National Socialists who also fought against the 'internationalists' and organized a Czech nationalistic, anti-Semitic, terrorist party.

By the same token, the extreme German nationalistic press presented rather strange theories about the differences between strong and weak human races and pleaded in favour of a pure Aryan race which deserved to regain the control over a world that allegedly had been taken over by the Jews.

Typical of this vision were the writings of Jörg Lanz von Liebenfels, a pan-German, who published, for example, a pamphlet entitled 'Race and Welfare Work'. In this pamphlet he tried to prove that at least a third of all diseases were caused by racial factors: 'All these disgusting diseases are of eastern origin and are basically diseases of dirt and race. The Aryan is afflicted by them as well, since he is compelled to be in contact with racially inferior people.'[7] Consequently, all those 'oriental' nations of a lower rank had to be isolated and treated as slaves.

Lanz coined the term of an allegedly 'evil race' and made it responsible for the spread of madness and sexual diseases. Therefore 'the state should pursue appropriate policies and eradicate families who are tainted by hereditary diseases. Hence, it would be possible to save a substantial amount of money spent on welfare.' In addition to this, he suggested granting welfare expenditure only to people 'with blond hair, blue (or grey-blue eyes), pink face colour, a long skull and face' and other racial distinctions such as 'a straight long nose, a well-proportioned mouth, with healthy white teeth, round chin and a tall figure, small hands and feet'. It is almost incomprehensible that contemporaries could take this seriously.

The Viennese writer Guido von List wrote several books, describing his vision of a future German global empire that would last at least a thousand years. However, as List argued, this could only be achieved if the Aryan race was purified of alien blood. He called it the 'Entmischung von Fremdvölkischen' ('demixing from alien peoples'), a term used later on in the Nazi totalitarian language. Moreover, List propagated the use of the swastika as a secret sign for identifying members of the secret societies which were to support his 'Aryan' philosophy.

But at the same time, the anti-Jewish agitation was not the only one directed against members of an allegedly inferior race. It went together with an ever increasing hatred against and contempt for most non-German nationalities, especially the Slavic peoples and also gypsies. In 1908, at a time when Hitler visited parliament, Dr Karl Iro, a prominent member of the pan-German faction and editor of the *Alldeutsches Tagblatt*, called for a law to legalize the arrest of all gypsies in order for them to be put into special camps. Their property and their children should be taken away from them. Moreover, Iro proposed that they should be tattooed with a certain number on their arms below the elbow to facilitate their identification. As is well known, the gypsies were the first to be tattooed in Auschwitz in exactly this way.

This proposal was immediately rejected by the parliamentary majority. But it is worth mentioning that these extremist racial concepts were loudly articulated in pre-war Vienna, despite the fact that the parliamentary representation of the pan-German movement was very small and even decreased after the turn of the century.

The most important political model for Hitler was Dr Karl Lueger, the leader of the Christian-Socialist Party, who ruled the city of Vienna from 1897 to 1910 as mayor. Hitler admired Lueger as the most successful populist politician of his time and praised him in long passages in *Mein Kampf* as the 'greatest mayor of all time'.[8] Actually, Lueger appeared as the man who represented the interests of the common people, and they regarded him as a popular hero, who was even more cherished than the Emperor Francis Joseph. Lueger had made his career by engaging himself for the needs of the lower middle classes in Vienna, who found themselves in a rather stressful situation during this period. By about 1910, only one third of the inhabitants of Vienna had been born in the city, and nearly two-thirds had migrated to the capital, mostly from Bohemia, but also from Hungary, Galicia or the Bukovina. The second biggest group among them were the Jews.

According to the emancipation laws introduced in 1867 all migrants from the Habsburg lands, whatever their nationality or religion, were citizens with equal rights. Many among them had remarkable careers, which were the cause of envy and scorn by the native population which remained behind and could not compete with the 'intruders'.

As mayor, Lueger tried to solve the immense problem of mass migration by enforcing the assimilation of especially Bohemian migrants. He urged them to become 'good' Germans and Viennese citizens, as his famous utterance 'Laßt mir meine Böhm in Ruh!' (Leave my Bohemia alone!) impressively shows. However, if they were not willing to become Germans and preferred to remain Czechs, they had to suffer extreme discrimination by the all-powerful city authorities.

As far as the Jews were concerned, Lueger relied on the *received* Christian anti-Semitism in order to isolate those Jews who did stay within their Mosaic religion. The question of the degree to which religious and racial anti-Semitism tended to merge cannot be answered easily. However, there exist clear indications that increasing parts of the Christian-Socialist movement, including a great many Catholic priests supporting Lueger, also embraced racial anti-Semitic feelings.

As a populist Lueger played on the fears and frustrations of the people of Vienna and constructed the fiction that 'the Jew' was the common enemy. He declared the Jewish tradesmen responsible for high prices or, when suitable, too low prices, and propagated a boycott of Jewish shops with the slogan 'Kauft nicht bei Juden!' – 'Don't buy from Jews!' He declared the Jewish students responsible for over-crowding in the universities, the Jewish sick for overcrowding in hospitals, and so on. In the Christian-Socialist propaganda Jewish artists and scientists were criticized for promoting the immorality allegedly inherent in contemporary art and science.

Denouncing all these degenerate influences, Lueger and his party followers called for a 'judenfreies Wien', a Vienna without Jews, and promised that all imminent social and economic problems might be settled after the Jews had been expelled. The anti-Semitic appeal worked quite successfully, and the Viennese population was frenzied in its admiration for the 'Herrgott von Wien', as they would call their adored mayor.

The language used by the Christian-Socialists appears to be rather brutal and fulfilled all the criteria of what Daniel Goldhagen would later on call 'eliminatory' anti-Semitism. For instance, Ernst Schneider, a Christian-Socialist member of parliament, proposed to put the Jews all together into a large ship, to steer it into the open sea and sink it there. If he could be sure that the very last Jew underwent the same fate, he himself would like to be drowned for rendering the best conceivable service to the world, an utterance which found amused agreement amongst his party friends.[9]

At the same time, the Catholic priest Joseph Scheicher, a prominent member of the Christian-Socialist party, was dreaming of a future Vienna without Jews, ruled by a strong catholic authority that would prohibit Jewish influence in the arts and the sciences and expel all democrats. The Catholic Church, in Scheicher's view, therefore had the right to exert its power without the interference of parliamentary acts.[10] In accordance with ideas like these, the Christian-Socialist newspapers would not hesitate to equate Jews with non-human beings and call them parasites, wolves, grasshoppers, insects which had to be poisoned by insect powder.[11] We might cite any number of further examples.

On the whole, Hitler's Vienna was a virtual panopticon of unstable spirits and nationalist fanatics, represented by personalities of divergent political persuasions, frequently quarrelling against each other: for example, as Wolf versus Stein, Schönerer versus Wolf, and all three against Lueger. Later on, Hitler was clever enough to exploit all these divergent traditions and to avoid the tactical errors of his Viennese idols.

But it must be stressed that during this period politics did not have any priority in Hitler's interests and predilections, as he did not want to enter a political career, and was still hoping to become a leading architect. On account of his excellent memory, he would learn the details of the buildings on the Ringstrasse, their dimensions in metres and centimetres, and recollected all these figures even as Reich chancellor. He was primarily concerned with musical and theatrical events, and especially interested in stage scenery. He drafted stage pictures for Wagner's operas and was eager to collect technical details of stage lighting and other effects, and even tried to compose an opera entitled *Wieland der Schmied* as a late completion of Wagner's plans. He was keen to learn and so pursued what he called his private studies, and indeed the amount of literature read by him in the Viennese years is highly impressive.

Undoubtedly, the four political idols of the young Hitler were extreme anti-Semites. Moreover, during his Viennese period he learnt all the common phrases of the anti-Semitic discourse of his time, which he would constantly use later on as a politician. In *Mein Kampf* he maintained that he had become an anti-Semite during his Vienna period.

This, however, appears to be dishonest. Surprisingly, Hitler entertained regular and continuous contacts with Jews, even with Jewish friends during his time in Vienna. First, there is the question of his relations with Dr Eduard Bloch, the Jewish doctor who tended Hitler's mother during her long illness, accompanying her even to death, as a close acquaintance of the whole family. The American psychohistorian Rudolf Binion developed the idea that Dr Bloch treated Hitler's mother with a painful, misguided method, and in addition to that, was too expensive. As a consequence, Hitler would hate Jews for the rest of his life.[12] The truth is the opposite. The young Hitler adored the doctor and often expressed his gratitude by sending him cards he had painted and similar gifts. After the *Anschluß* of Austria to the German Reich in 1938, Dr Bloch, who had written some letters to Hitler for help, was the only Austrian Jew who stood under the protection of the Gestapo and was allowed to emigrate with his fortune to America. In his memoirs, published in an American newspaper in 1941,[13] Bloch displayed a surprisingly positive evaluation of the young Hitler and his Linz family. He mentioned Hitler's deep love of and attachment towards his mother in particular[14] and took care to note that Hitler, who was then 18 years old, was not yet infected by anti-Semitism. Or in his own words: 'He had not yet begun to hate the Jews'.

Another example of an erroneous interpretation is the assumption that Hitler's anti-Semitism became virulent when he failed to pass his examinations at the Academy of Arts in Vienna on account of Jewish professors.[15] But none of the teachers in question were Jewish or of Jewish descent, and the actual professor who refused Hitler's entry into the academy turned out to be the Christian Griepenkerl, a rather old man of a fairly conservative artistic style, who came from Oldenburg in northern Germany. None of the theories that Hitler's anti-Semitism was a result of bad personal experiences with Jews in Vienna can be proved.

The young Hitler had many, quite friendly relations with Jews, despite all his reading of anti-Semitic books and newspapers. Thus he admired Gustav Mahler as the ideal conductor of Wagner's operas and did not join the anti-Semitic uproar against Mahler in Vienna.

With his friend Kubizek Hitler went to a house of the rich Jewish factory-owner Dr Rudolf Jahoda, where Kubizek played the viola in weekly house concerts. Hitler was deeply impressed by the cultured atmosphere and especially the rich library, and did not utter any word in this (or in any other) context against this visit.

In the men's hostel he preferred Jewish friends. The closest one was Josef Neumann, a hawker, who helped him selling his pictures. Neumann gave him a worn suit as a present because Hitler was so poor that he lacked sufficient clothing through the winter. With Neumann he engaged in discussions about Jews, and obviously under his influence he opposed anti-Semitic lodgers in the hostel. He defended Heinrich Heine, praised Mendelssohn and Offenbach as composers, and even quoted Lessing's ring parable maintaining the equality of the three religions.[16]

Hitler's Jewish fellow-traveller Siegfried Löffner sold his paintings too, and even induced the police to have Hitler's enemy Reinhold Hanisch arrested. Moreover, the one-eyed locksmith Simon Robinson from Galicia lent Hitler, who frequently ran out of money, some of his small disability rent. Proof of the Jewish religion of these friends is found in the documents of the registration office in Vienna.

Moreover, the tradesmen who bought Hitler's paintings for a quite reasonable price were thoroughly Jewish. One of them, Jacob Altenberg from Galicia, said afterwards that he never heard any anti-Semitic utterance from Hitler. In fact, Hitler did not hesitate to entertain relations with Jews. The closest relation Hitler had with Jewish partners was that with a Viennese Jew called Samuel Morgenstern, who happened to be a glazier, and his wife. In this case, Hitler who otherwise shied away from contacts with customers, did not hesitate to visit them almost every week for several years. A letter sent by Morgenstern to Hitler in 1939 never reached him, and he and his wife were deported to Lodz and afterwards to Auschwitz. Another example reached me after having finished my book. The son of a former houseowner in the Stumpergasse told me that the young Hitler would go every morning to a Jewish distiller (*Branntweiner*) near his flat to have a small breakfast there consisting always of 'a tea and a kipfel'. And he did this even though there were many non-Jewish coffeeshops in the neighbourhood. Research in the registration office in Vienna revealed that this distiller was Simon Wasserberg, born in Galicia, 'religion: Mosaic'. After 1938, Wasserberg could not understand why his former client changed his mind so completely. The distiller ended up as an old man in Theresienstadt.

In conclusion, it must be emphasised that during his Vienna years, one cannot discover any obvious anti-Semitic utterance by Hitler, while he strongly criticized the Social Democrats, the Catholic Church, the Jesuits and the Habsburg dynasty.

These findings, however, do not coincide with the report presented by Hitler's former friend August Kubizek, who already knew Hitler from the Linz period and lived in one room together with him for some months. In a book which he published in 1953,[17] Kubizek decribes Hitler's anti-Semitic leanings from the Linz period onwards in a rather detailed way. Although most of Kubizek's recollections appear to be correct, his assumptions relating to Hitler's anti-Semitism obviously do not coincide with all the other recollections of Viennese eyewitnesses. But there is a simple biographical explanation for this special case.

Before he wrote his book Kubizek, whose close relations to Hitler became known to the occupying powers, spent sixteen months in American custody. Here he was also accused of being an anti-Semite. Hence he defended himself by arguing that the 18-year-old Hitler had compelled him to join the Austrian Anti-Semitic Union. But this union, being founded in 1919, did not exist in 1908. This and some other arguments make it unmistakably clear that Kubizek's accusations in this respect were a means of self-protection.

There can be no doubt that Hitler, although being confronted with anti-Semitic pamphlets and slogans all the time, did not engage in any clashes or conflicts or gain other negative experiences with Jews. There exists an obvious contradiction between his personal life style and the absorption of the pan-German and Christian-socialist anti-Semitic propaganda. It seems that the change of his general political views into active political strategies did not occur, as far as anti-Semitism is concerned, before his experiences during and after the First World War.

It seems likely that Hitler took the notion of using anti-Semitic prejudices for mass agitation from Karl Lueger. From his very beginnings in Vienna he learnt to conceive political issues and structures mainly from a visionary and utopian standpoint. During his Vienna years anti-Semitism was only one of many unsystematically absorbed ideas. And even during the first year in Munich, Rudolf Häusler couldn't detect any sign of a personal anti-Semitism in his close friend Hitler.

In consequence of these findings, the question remains: when did Hitler become an anti-Semite, if not as a young man in Vienna and in Munich until August 1914, when Häusler left him to return to Vienna? The only possibility for change is the experience of the First World War – again a period where biographical references about Hitler are few and far between – and at the latest the period of 1918/19 when he went public as an aggressive anti-Semitic politician. There is indeed still a lot of work to be done by the historians.

Notes

1. Brigitte Hamann, *Hitlers Wien: Lehrjahre eine Diktators*. English Translation: *Hitler's Vienna: A Dictator's Apprenticeship* (Oxford 1999).
2. Adolf Hitler, *Mein Kampf*, einbändige Volksausgabe, München 1940, 1–137.
3. Reinhold Hanisch, 'I was Hitler's Buddy', *The New Republic*, 5, 2 and 19 April, 1939.
4. Konrad Heiden, *Adolf Hitler*, Zürich 1936.
5. Karl Honisch, Protokoll, 12 July, 1939. Deutsches Bundesarchiv Koblenz BA, NS 26/17a.
6. Josef Greiner, *Das Ende des Hitler-Mythos*, Wien 1947. Hamann, 275–80.
7. Jörg Lanz-Liebenfels, *Rasse und Wohlfahrtspflege*, Wien 1907.
8. Hitler, *Mein Kampf*, 59.
9. Rudolf Kuppe, *Karl Lueger und seine Zeit*, Wien 1933, 216f.
10. Joseph Scheicher, *Aus dem Jahre 1920. Ein Traum*, St Pölten 1900.
11. Hamann, 413ff.

12. Rudolf Binion, *Hitler among the Germans*, New York 1976.
13. Dr Eduard Bloch, as told to J. D. Ratcliff, 'My Patient Hitler', *Collier's*, 15 and 22 March, 1941.
14. That means, too, that the thesis accepted by many biographers that Hitler had left his dying mother alone and had refused to come to Linz before she died, as Bradley F. Smith and many of his followers such as Joachim Fest argue, is not true, as this relies on the dubious information given by Franz Jetzinger, *Hitler's Jugend*, Wien 1956, 176ff. Bradley F. Smith, *Adolf Hitler. His family, Childhood and Youth*. Stanford 1967, 112. Hamann, 83–6.
15. J. Sidney Jones, *Hitlers Weg began in Wien*. Wiesbaden 1980, 317.
16. Hamann, 499 after Hanisch.
17. August Kubiek, *Adolf Hitler. Mein Jugendfreund*, Graz 1953.

WOLFGANG SCHIEDER

Fatal Attraction: The German Right and Italian Fascism

There was no contemporary politician Hitler venerated more than Benito Mussolini,[1] Italy's Fascist dictator. It was no accident that Hitler's only two state visits were to Italy in 1934 and 1938. In his early days, he admired the Italian's 'outstanding genius'.[2] Even in periods of strained German–Italian relations, Hitler still found reasons for exempting Mussolini from his general criticism of Fascism. Just before Mussolini's downfall, Hitler maintained that within Fascism 'only the Duce has stayed true to himself'.[3] While judging the alliance with Italy a political mistake, Hitler in his last days is said to have asserted that his 'personal affection for the Duce' remained unchanged.[4]

How can we explain this peculiar attachment? So far, historians have tended to neglect this question. The mutual respect of both Fascist dictators was taken for granted. It seemed to flow almost naturally from ideological affinities or from the constraints of foreign politics. Some historians – let me just name Renzo De Felice – have concentrated on the differences between both dictators, not those things they held in common. Indeed, more than once Mussolini spoke negatively about Hitler. Still, it remains true that the German regarded the Italian as his political mentor till the end of his life. Therefore Hitler's high regard for Mussolini calls for an explanation.

My attempt at such an explanation rests on three arguments, which I would like to develop in this chapter: First, I shall try to show that Hitler admired Mussolini as a successful power politician. Since 1922, Hitler was fascinated by the way Mussolini and his Fascist mass movement came to power.

But Hitler was not only *impressed* by Mussolini's political strategy. My second argument is that Hitler up to 1933 consciously *imitated*

Mussolini's strategy, of course adapted to the German situation. It was the Fascist example that inspired Hitler on his way to power.[5]

Thirdly, to me there is no doubt that Hitler's rise to power would not have occurred so easily without Mussolini's precedent. Hitler's success rested on the public impression – carefully supported by Hitler himself – that he planned to do in Germany what Mussolini had done in Italy. This made him seem a serious, even welcome, political option in Germany, where Mussolini's Fascist regime enjoyed remarkable popularity.[6]

In no other contemporary European country was so much written about Fascism as in Germany. Between 1922 and 1933, almost 200 books and several thousand articles in newspapers and journals were published about the 'Italian experiment', to use a term coined by the economist Erwin von Beckerath.[7] It is even more important to note that this wave of interest in Fascism was not restricted to mere academic discourse. In fact, the German discussion of Fascism reflected the crisis of the Weimar Republic. After Mussolini had consolidated his dictatorial leadership in 1925, after the Carta del Lavoro of 1927 seemed to offer a corporatist economic model against class warfare, and finally, after Mussolini had made his peace with the Vatican in the Lateran Treaties of 1929, the Fascist regime met with widespread approval in Germany.[8] The nationalist writer Moeller van den Bruck found the compelling formula: 'Italia docet'.[9] During the crisis years of Weimar party government, Fascist dictatorship seemed a viable political alternative to a discredited parliamentary system. This facilitated Hitler's strategy of shaping himself into a German Mussolini.

Of course the Weimar Republic did not lack people who warned against transferring the Fascist model to Germany. They were especially to be found on the political Left. Famous journals of the democratic Left, such as the *Weltbühne* or the *Tagebuch*, regularly dealt with the attraction of Italian Fascism. But for these journals Fascism did not seem to be different from any other dictatorial system. The journalists writing for them therefore underestimated the danger of transferring Fascism to Germany.[10]

The same can be said, with different reasons, of the Communists. By integrating Fascism into the Leninist concept of class struggle, Fascism appeared to be a necessary outgrowth of the capitalist system. But instead of strengthening an anti-Fascist attitude, this analysis tended to limit the impact of Communist anti-Fascism. Communist anti-Fascism was not specifically directed against National Socialism, but opposed the entire 'bourgeoisie', of which Fascism only seemed to be the vanguard.[11] Thus, the Communists were unable to see the real danger arising from Hitler.

Many Social Democrats, too, tried to reassure themselves by asserting that 'Germany is not Italy'.[12] This statement even applies to the most astute contemporary observer of Italian Fascism, a professor of law, Hermann Heller. In his 1929 book *Europe and Fascism*,[13] he painted 'Fascist dictatorship' as a 'frightful example' to European democracies.[14] He attributed the rise of National Socialism to the same social roots that had motivated the rise of Fascism in Italy. Still, he would not believe in the political success of National Socialism. In Heller's opinion, Fascist dictatorship was closely linked to Mussolini's charismatic personality. This, Heller thought, could not be imitated. For him, Hitler merely appeared to be 'a sad copy of Mussolini'.[15]

Heller's misjudgement proved particularly damaging. Because of his academic authority, it became common opinion among German Social Democrats. As late as 8 February 1933, the Social Democratic Party journal *Vorwärts* proclaimed: 'Berlin is not Rome. Hitler is not Mussolini. Berlin will never be the capital of a Fascist empire. Berlin will always stay red.'[16] Despite recognizing the political clout of Italy's Fascism, the leading elites of social democracy tended to overestimate their own political weight. The belief in the 'historic laws' of class struggle did not permit the admission that social democracy was politically powerless against a mass movement that enjoyed widespread popular support, although it was marked by a basic counter-revolutionary impulse.

The political miscalculations of the majority of Fascism's German enemies would have been less grave, if Mussolini's message had met with no further response in the Weimar Republic. Unfortunately, the opposite was the case. Fascism as a topic of discussion was never restricted to the political Left. On the contrary, the political Right in Germany showed more interest in Fascism than the Left and created a climate of opinion that became increasingly philo-Fascist during the final years of the Weimar Republic. Compared to the philo-Fascism prevailing in public opinion, the Left's criticism of Fascism was basically condemned to stay ineffectual. Although Italy's policy in the South Tyrol met with strong nationalist reservations among the German middle classes, Fascism enjoyed a remarkable increase in approval towards the end of the Weimar Republic. The more the German republic drifted into crisis, the more Fascism was politically appreciated.

However, to judge this rise in appreciation and approval properly, it is important to understand that the Fascist phenomenon was by no means understood in its entirety. On the contrary, the German discussion was characterized by a 'selective reading' of Fascism. Certain elements of Fascist rule were singled out for enthusiastic praise, while others were not perceived or explored at all. The most remarkable example is the almost total neglect of the regime's background in a reign of terror.

An important reason for this neglect was Mussolini's cunning way of presenting himself and of influencing public opinion in Germany. Among the major instruments in creating the image of statesmanship were private receptions and audiences, which could always be sure of prominent coverage in German newspapers.[17] Leading middle-class journalists were found competing for appointments and private interviews with Mussolini in the Palazzo Venezia in Rome. One after the other would succumb to Mussolini's carefully arranged performances. For a start, an interview was only granted after a considerable period of time. Having secured an appointment, the lucky guest was summoned for an hour well before Mussolini was prepared to see him or her. This first of all meant waiting in one of Mussolini's ante-chambers, where the guest was presented with a show of bustling activity: busy secretaries, military officers or Fascist dignitaries in black uniform were paraded to impress the visitor. All of a sudden came the summons into Mussolini's room. Typically, the dictator would wait behind his desk at the end of the room, while the visitor had to pass 25 metres along a polished marble floor, before reaching the desk. Only then would Mussolini invite the guest to take a seat.

Mussolini usually proved well-prepared for the subsequent interview, surprising German visitors by addressing them in their mother tongue. Invariably, it was Mussolini, not the visitor, who determined the topic and course of the conversation. Little surprise that at the end of the interview his visitors tended to be entirely captivated by the dictator!

The writers Emil Ludwig and Theodor Wolff provide two particularly telling examples. Both can be numbered among the most prominent democratic journalists of the Weimar Republic, and both originally had criticized the Fascist dictatorial system. Given this background, an article by Wolff in the *Berliner Tageblatt* of 11 May 1930 created a considerable sensation. Following an interview in Rome, Wolff described Mussolini as a moderate and realistic politician without 'nationalist conceit'.[18] Indeed, Wolff in his interview had made an attempt at mentioning the suppression of Italy's opposition, but he did not question Mussolini's explanation that this conduct was necessary for the establishment of an 'authoritarian democracy'.[19]

Even greater was the public impact of a series of interviews which Emil Ludwig had held with Mussolini between 23 March and 4 April 1932. The resulting book, *Mussolini's Interviews with Emil Ludwig*, was translated into seven languages and became a sort of political bestseller in Germany during 1932.[20] Ludwig was straightforward in his praise for Mussolini as a 'great statesman' and a 'true dictator'. Moreover, he credited Mussolini with being a 'man of most exquisite courtesy' and one of 'the most natural people in the world'.[21] Like Wolff, Ludwig claims to have discussed the 'dangers of dictatorship' with Mussolini, but on the whole Ludwig's book leaves the impression that the 'constructive elements' in Mussolini's dictatorship far outweighed its negative characteristics.[22]

Both Wolff and Ludwig made it clear to their readers that it was the crisis of the Republic that had caused the change in their political sentiments. To them, the *temporary* establishment of an authoritarian regime based on the Fascist model seemed to offer a political way out of the precarious situation in Germany.

At the same time, both writers stressed the differences between Mussolini's Fascism and its 'German imitators'.[23] They were satisfied with Mussolini's statement that he did not recognize his self-proclaimed supporters outside Italy. Even though Mussolini started a pan-Fascist initiative about this time, both writers felt assured by his assertion that the Italian breed of Fascism was 'no article for export'.[24] Both Wolff and Ludwig being of Jewish descent, they put special emphasis on the absence of anti-Semitism from Italian Fascism. In their eyes, this constituted an indisputable difference from National Socialism, which they continued to fight vehemently. During a talk with Victor Klemperer, the scholar and famous diarist, Wolff said in May 1932: 'Mussolini does not care that someone is a Jew, he is different from Hitler, he preserves order and does not torment anybody who does not systematically oppose him! In short: if only we had a German Mussolini!'[25]

This attitude towards Fascism symbolizes a central feature of philo-Fascist tendencies in Germany: admiration or praise for Mussolini need not necessarily imply support for Hitler. As far as the objectives of Mussolini's admirers are concerned, it might rather mean the exact opposite: support for Fascism might underline reservations about National Socialism. This can be seen in the way Fascism was considered

by German industrialists and business leaders. Up to the end of the
1920s, Fascism was not a prominent subject of debate within employers'
associations, and there are certainly no signs of approval. This situation
changed, however, when the first stirrings of the Great Depression
were felt about 1929/30. Now, Fascist corporatism seemed to offer an
attractive vision of a new economic order, and widespread discussion
of corporatism's merits and prospects commenced among industrialists
and economic writers. An important role in propagating corporatist
ideas was played by the writer Hans Reupke. The Reichsverband der
deutschen Industrie (National Association of German Industry) even
granted him money to spend a period of research in Italy. The result
was Reupke's book of 1930, *The Economic System of Fascism*.[26] In this
book, Reupke characterized Fascism as the 'pioneer of the capitalist
system'.[27] He accorded special emphasis to the wide scope for private
initiative which he saw preserved in Fascist corporatism. This promis-
ing analysis even aroused interest among industrialists who usually
distrusted National *Socialism*.

What Mussolini's Corporatism was for industrialists, Mussolini's
relations with the Catholic Church were for politicians and journalists
around the Catholic Centre Party. This had not always been the case.
During the first years of the Weimar Republic, political Catholicism
in Germany had taken a very reserved view of Fascism. Mussolini's
policy towards South Tyrol as well as the dictatorial consolidation of
the Fascist regime – in particular the ban on the Partito Popolare
Italiano in 1926 – had kept relations between politicians from the
Centre Party and Mussolini cool and reserved. However, this changed
rapidly with the Lateran Treaties and the Concordat between Italy
and the Vatican in 1929. Few of the public spokesmen of political
Catholicism now maintained their rejection of Fascism, while the
majority of Catholic politicians and journalists renounced their
reservations about Mussolini. For the first time, they accepted the
Fascist dictator as the 'man of providence' (Pius XI).

The conduct of Cologne mayor Konrad Adenauer is typical of the
changed attitude of political Catholicism towards Mussolini. 'As a
Catholic', he not only congratulated the papal Nuncio in Germany,
Pacelli, on the signing of the Lateran Treaties, but he also sent a
complimentary telegram to Mussolini.[28] In an interview with the
Fascist Carlo Scorza in 1932, he praised Mussolini's statesmanship
with explicit reference to his reconciliation with the Vatican.[29]

However, equally characteristic is Adenauer's conviction that the
establishment of a regime based on the Fascist model was inconceivable

outside Italy. This agreed with the predominant interpretation of Fascism within German political Catholicism after 1929. Reich Chancellor Brüning, himself a protagonist of the Catholic Right, also seems to have been affected by the 'Mussolini-craze' in the Catholic camp. When writing his memoirs in the 1940s, he still counted his state visit to Italy in August 1931 among 'the few pleasant recollections of these hard times'.[30]

The attitude found among leading politicians from the Centre Party featured even more strongly among Catholic political journalists. During the crisis years of the Weimar Republic, we can observe a kind of Catholic anti-Nazism, which originated in a feeling of affinity with Italian Fascism. A pivotal role in this context was played by Edmund Freiherr Raitz von Frentz, the Rome correspondent of four important German Catholic newspapers.[31] Even in periods of conflict between the Vatican and the Fascist regime after 1929, this journalist continued to point out the political gains from the Concordat and the Lateran Treaties. To Raitz, the positive Fascist attitude towards the Church seemed to reveal the fundamental difference between Mussolini and Hitler. Therefore Raitz persistently appealed to the Catholic public not to reject Fascism just because it might be claimed as an inspiration by National Socialists.[32]

Enthusiasm for Mussolini, based on a 'selective reading' of his politics, was even more common in the pages of Catholic journals than in the daily press of the Centre Party. Although the writers of these journals typically formed a self-centred circle of intellectuals that seldom crossed the boundaries into a wider public, the enthusiasm for Mussolini expressed in Catholic journals appears extraordinarily marked. For example, in 1926 the young writer Eugen Kogon enthused about the corporatist economic system outlined in the Charter of Labour. He hoped that 'Fascism would prove to be a crucial phenomenon of the century'.[33] One Franconian cleric, Georg Moenius, in his journal *Schönere Zukunft* (A Brighter Future), even propagated Italian Fascism as a Catholic programme for dictatorship. Mussolini was celebrated as an incarnation of Latin-Roman and Catholic-Christian traditions, which were seen to be entirely different from the anti-Roman Catholic and Germanic-pagan rites of National Socialism. Consequently, Moenius deprecated National Socialism as 'German pseudo-Fascism', which was fundamentally different from 'true Fascism originating in the Catholic spirit'.[34] Thus, in Catholic journals Mussolini was presented as the man who had achieved the political reconciliation of State and Catholic Church – a task considered to be impossible for National Socialism.

This kind of propaganda for Mussolini, based on approval of his policy towards the Church, was a speciality of political Catholicism. It did not find a parallel on the Protestant side, which at any rate did not present an equally united front. Still, due to the activities of conservative spokesmen with a Protestant background, Mussolini achieved the same popularity among Protestant conservatives as on the other side of the confessional divide.

Again, this result could not be taken for granted. The rejection of Mussolini's policy in the South Tyrol carried special weight with a German Right rooted in nationalist and conservative traditions. Mussolini's secret attempts at talks with representatives of the Deutschnationale Volkspartei (German Nationalist Party) and the Reichswehr failed completely in 1924. Furthermore, nationalistic and conservative reservations about Fascism were confirmed when the German–Italian conflict over South Tyrol broke out in February 1926. Only when the crisis of the Weimar Republic came to a head towards the end of the 1920s, did the reservations from the Right about the Fascist regime gradually subside. Now the authoritarian character of Mussolini's regime was attractive for many observers in the conservative camp.

It is interesting to note that in the process of rapprochement between conservatives and Fascism, certain monarchist members of the high aristocracy took the political lead. In the first place, Philipp Prince of Hesse has to be named. Married to a daughter of King Vittorio Emmanuele III, he acted as a discreet go-between in Rome and established a number of political contacts.[35] One of the people taken in by Mussolini after an audience was former crown prince Frederick of Hohenzollern. In a letter to his father in May 1928, he complained about the 'unbelievable short-sightedness in nationally minded circles'. He accused them of being hoodwinked by the 'propagandist clamour of our democratic press' into attacking Mussolini for his policy towards South Tyrol. Instead, the former crown prince was full of admiration for Mussolini's 'ingenious brutality' in suppressing socialism, democracy and Freemasonry.[36]

However, among the various conservative groups it was the Stahlhelm, a paramilitary association of veterans from the First World War, that took the most decided pro-Fascist course. It was not so much Fascism's ideology that appealed to the Stahlhelm, as its political style. As early as 1925, the journalist Helmut Franke had been to Rome.[37] Subsequently, this writer, who professed to work for a 'national revolution', tried to commit the Stahlhelm to Fascism, praising the latter as a new nationalism of a kindred spirit. At first, Franke's initiative proved a failure. The *Stahlhelm*'s leadership in the twenties hesitated to adopt a course that would take the 'oppressor of *Deutschtum* [German civilization]' in South Tyrol as its precedent. Franke and other supporters of a 'national revolution' were pushed out of the association.[38]

In the development of the Stahlhelm's relations with Fascism, Hitler's victory in the general elections of September 1930 proved the turning point. From the success of the NSDAP, Mussolini drew the conclusion that Germany was ripe for dictatorship. He now devoted special attention to the Stahlhelm. His interest was motivated partly by his concern that Hitler in particular would benefit from the changed situation in Germany, partly by his conviction that Hitler would not be able to move into the centre of power on his own. Step by step, contacts between the Stahlhelm and the Partito Nazionale Fascista were intensified during 1930/1. The sixteenth of November 1930 marked a first climax when the association's journal *Der Stahlhelm* gave pride of place to a front-page article on 'Italy and Germany'. The article was written by Giuseppe Renzetti, Mussolini's still mysterious personal agent in Berlin.[39] This was no accident, as Renzetti from 1930 onwards became a key figure in propagating Fascism in Germany. It is no exaggeration to state that without Renzetti's activities, German discussions of Fascism would never have achieved the political quality that was necessary to make Fascism the role-model and precedent for the right-wing enemies of the Weimar Republic. In the early 1920s, Renzetti had taken the initiative in establishing a German–Italian Chamber of Commerce in Berlin. At the same time he acted as representative of the *Fasci all'estero* in Germany. From the end of the 1920s, he moved easily among the German Right. His activities paid off after the general elections of September 1930. In July of that year, he had been almost alone among contemporary observers to predict a result of more than 100 parliamentary seats for the National Socialists. This accurate prediction secured him Mussolini's special attention, and from the end of 1930 onwards almost all Fascist contacts to leading National Socialists were arranged by Renzetti.[40]

Originally, Renzetti had singled out the Stahlhelm as the appropriate partner for Fascism. Completely underestimating this paramilitary association's political weakness, he believed he was dealing with the core troops of a future dictatorship based on the Fascist model.[41] Direct contacts between the Stahlhelm and leading Fascists were meant to speed up the ideological penetration of the association and to make it break away from the anti-Italian phalanx on the German Right. From 1931 onwards, Renzetti's persistent activities resulted in a growing number of visits by Stahlhelm leaders to Italy. The Fascist congress celebrating the tenth anniversary of the March on Rome provided the occasion for the 'highlight' among these philo-Fascist visits: in November 1932, Stahlhelm leader Franz Seldte was granted a reception by Mussolini.[42]

The Stahlhelm leadership may have been little interested in the political content of Fascist ideology, but it is undeniably true that the association's closer ties with Fascism contributed to the Stahlhelm's decision to seek cooperation with the National Socialists. This move was motivated by a political calculation based on the idea that Hitler as well as Hindenburg and the Reichswehr might be integrated into a Fascist-conservative regime similar to Mussolini's rule in Italy.

With historical hindsight it might seem evident that the political group in Germany closest to Fascism were the National Socialists. On closer inspection, however, it emerges that the cooperation between both right-wing movements cannot be taken for granted. National Socialism had developed independently from Fascism, and its opening up to Fascist influences proved an extremely protracted process. Prior to 1933, three main obstacles prevented both an open alliance with Fascism and its conscious imitation: First, the Fascist policy of repression in the formerly Austrian region of South Tyrol; secondly, the absence of anti-Semitism from Fascist ideology; and thirdly, the conception that Fascism lacked the will to effect a thorough change in the social and economic system. It is mainly due to Hitler that these obstacles were overcome. Despite reluctance and criticism from inside his party, he decided at an early date to pursue a pro-Fascist course and openly to play the Fascist card on his way to power.

In 1919, the National Socialists still shared the anti-Italian attitude of all German parties on the issue of South Tyrol.[43] A party like the NSDAP, with its deep roots in nationalist sentiment, could not stand to one side when all Germany denounced the suppression of South Tyrol by the Italian 'traitors'.[44] This only changed when Hitler's attention was drawn to Mussolini a few months before the Fascists' March on Rome. In September 1922, Hitler dispatched a certain Kurt Ludecke to Rome, suggesting a cooperation between National Socialism and Fascism.[45]

However, at this point the Nazi position on South Tyrol precluded any common initiatives between both movements. Still, Hitler saw his regard for Mussolini confirmed by the March on Rome. Diverging from the path of all other political parties in Germany, Hitler now decided to recognize Italy's annexation of South Tyrol.

Hitler only publicized his change of opinion during the German–Italian conflict on South Tyrol at the beginning of 1926, when he published a pamphlet entitled *The Question of South Tyrol and the German Problem of Alliances*.[46] But even from inside his own party, Hitler had to face strong objections to his change of course. Returning from 'our German South Tyrol' and getting hold of Hitler's pamphlet, Hans Frank temporarily left the NSDAP.[47] In the *Völkischer Beobachter*, Rosenberg continued for years to grumble about the Fascists' 'violent attempts' at integrating South Tyrol into the Italian nation.[48] Rosenberg found it hard to adjust to Hitler's prescribed phraseology on the subject.

It also took Goebbels some time to get used to Hitler's new, pro-Italian course. After a visit to Andreas Hofer's tomb in the Innsbruck Hofkirche (court chapel), Goebbels wrote as late as August 1928: 'The Italian is a bastard, after all – with the exception of Mussolini!'[49] It was only this admiration for Mussolini himself, emphatically praised as his 'great contemporary role-model', that moved Goebbels to accept Italy's policies in South Tyrol.[50]

Hermann Göring was the only leading National Socialist who had no qualms whatsoever about Hitler's policy towards Italy. Exiled in Sweden, Göring published three long articles in the *Völkischer Beobachter* of March 1926, entitled 'On the German–Italian Conflict'.[51] These articles attributed the strains in Italian–German relations to the French influence on the peace settlements of 1919. By assigning South Tyrol to Italy, the French in Göring's opinion had cleverly managed to establish a permanent point of contention between both countries. Against current feelings, Göring claimed the existence of a community of interests between the German and Italian peoples. These common interests, however, could only come to the fore once Mussolini would deal with a future 'nationalist and *völkisch* government in Germany'.[52] In this context, Göring not only spoke of 'manifold family ties' between Italian Fascism and National Socialism,[53] he also raised Mussolini to the position of leader of an international *völkisch* movement: 'In the same way as Russia and Moscow are the Mecca for the faithful of international Communism, Italy and Rome act as example and role-model to the nationalist movements.'[54]

In line with this attitude, Göring was the first prominent National Socialist who sought to implement Hitler's new Italian policy in practical politics. Once more, it was Giuseppe Renzetti, who established contacts with Mussolini. Göring first met Renzetti at the beginning of 1929,[55] and it was the Italian agent who arranged Göring's visit to Rome in April 1931. Travelling on Hitler's special order and as his trusted representative, Göring for the first time conducted talks with Fascist party leaders and was granted an official audience with Mussolini. On his return to Germany, Göring presented Hitler with a political souvenir – a photo of Mussolini with an autograph signature. It is the first personal present we know from the Italian dictator to his German master pupil.[56]

Finally, Göring also was the first prominent National Socialist to find a propagandistically effective way of concealing differences between Fascism and National Socialism on the issue of anti-Semitism. As Göring argued in 1926, any 'semblance of differences in dealing with the race question' would disappear in the future. Fascism sooner or later would take up the 'fight against Jewry (*Judentum*)' since the Jews in Göring's opinion had already started to fight Fascism. In fact, with its ban on Freemasonry Göring saw Fascism on the right track – after all, the Freemasons were nothing but the 'Jewish chief of staff'.[57]

Apart from the position on South Tyrol, the National Socialists also were divided on the issue of Socialism. The party 'Left' in particular, which was centred on Gregor Strasser, criticized Fascism's social and economic programme. They never tired of pointing out the differences between National Socialism and Fascism on this issue.[58] The debate on the social and economic structure of the Fascist state was kindled by Hans Reupke's book *National Socialism and the Economy*.[59] Reupke argued that a future National Socialist government would have to follow Fascism in preserving the capitalist order, especially the right of private property. In Reupke's opinion, National Socialism had to renounce all socialist ideas and experiments. This caused vehement criticism from the party 'Left'. Future Gauleiter Erich Koch, for example, claimed a fundamental difference between the socio-economic orders of Fascism and National Socialism: for him, the former was capitalist, the latter socialist.[60]

However, despite manifold Nazi reservations about Fascism – concerning the issues of foreign politics, ideology of race and socio-economic vision – in the end Hitler's pro-Fascist course prevailed. Hitler's early political opting for Mussolini turned out to offer a viable political concept for a German road to Fascism.

In fact, Hitler never denied that he used Mussolini's strategy as a blueprint for his own way to power. As early as 8 November 1922, just a few days after the March on Rome, Hitler had himself celebrated in Munich as a German equivalent to 'Italy's Mussolini'.[61] And in June 1941, he explained during one of his notorious table talks that the March on Rome had been one of 'the turning points in history': 'The simple fact that it could be done served as an encouragement to us all.'[62]

In 1922, however, Hitler had only half grasped Mussolini's political strategy. His attempt to instigate a 'March on Berlin' ended with the dismal failure of the Beer Hall putsch in Munich on 9 November 1923. Only afterwards did Hitler come to understand that Mussolini had pursued a double-sided political strategy: while preparing his *coup d'état*, Mussolini had at the same time engaged in regular negotiations to form a coalition government. Significantly, after 1923 Hitler admitted planning a putsch as Mussolini had done, but he no longer justified his aim with a mere revolutionary will to power. Instead he promised to act like Mussolini in 'legalizing our actions' afterwards.[63]

In shaping his strategy, Hitler had to be much more careful than Mussolini not to drift into illegality. Still, repeated statements prove that Hitler's strategy for a seizure of power was fundamentally inspired by the Fascist model. This model provided a strategy that was both revolutionary and legal at the same time. When Hitler, for the first time, fancied himself within reach of power, he even mentioned the Italian precedent to Franz von Papen on 13 August 1932. Both men were negotiating a Nazi participation in government. In order to support his demand for the position of Reich Chancellor, Hitler referred to Mussolini, who after the March on Rome also had been granted 'comprehensive power' by the king. Hitler refused the offer to become Vice Chancellor and confirmed his resolution in the subsequent meeting with Reich President Hindenburg.

Again and again, Hitler criticized the reality of Fascism in Italy, in particular the permanent influence of Catholic Church, king and reactionary generals. But not only did he always exempt Mussolini from such criticism, he also stuck to his conviction that there was a fundamental 'common ground between the Fascist and the National Socialist revolutions'.[64] Mussolini, it might be said in conclusion, taught Hitler how to seize power, even if the political frameworks that allowed their success were different. After the seizure of power, Hitler more and more managed to shift the balance of power away from his nationalist and conservative allies to the National Socialists. The greater his success in this respect, the further his regime moved away from Mussolini's system. But up to 1933, the phrase 'Italia docet' offers an accurate description of the relations between Fascism and National Socialism.

Finally, I would like to ask to what extent Hitler in his seizure of power derived political benefit from the philo-Fascist climate in Germany, which undoubtedly had emerged by the early 1930s. Although it would be premature to attempt a comprehensive answer to this question, it is possible to draw some preliminary conclusions from the evidence I have presented in this chapter.

1   During the crisis of the Weimar party system, and after the fall of Reich Chancellor Brüning in May 1932 at the latest, people thought about substituting a formal dictatorship for the parliamentary-democratic constitution. In this situation, Mussolini's Fascist regime offered only one of several possible models for the intended change. As we know today, even in the desperate agonies of the late Weimar Republic, the establishment of a Fascist regime was never a matter of necessity. However, from autumn 1930 onwards, the Nazi mass movement had become a strong element in the power game and could not be ignored. As this movement showed the spirit of Fascism, and as Hitler openly played the Fascist card, a dictatorship based on the Italian model undoubtedly recommended itself to many as the most realistic way out of crisis.

2   Towards the end of the Weimar Republic, Italian Fascism was second to no other form of dictatorship in the acceptance it enjoyed from a wide range of political convictions. It is true that this approval was usually limited to certain aspects of Fascist government and ideology. But it was this very selectivity in the observation of Fascist reality that secured a peculiarly positive climate of opinion for Mussolini's regime. The more Hitler moulded his political strategy according to the political expectations thriving in this climate, the more he was able to profit from pro-Fascist sentiments.

3   In the long run, even widespread philo-Fascism with an anti-Nazi edge worked in Hitler's favour. To explore Fascism as an alternative to National Socialism still undermined public confidence in the values of liberal democracy.

If disgust at anti-Semitism only led to stronger affinities with Fascism, such behaviour weakened the Weimar Republic, but did nothing effective to fight anti-Semitism.

If support for Fascism was meant to be directed against Hitler's anti-religious and anti-ecclesiastical policies, the whole argument broke down as soon as Hitler sanctioned the idea of a Concordat with the Vatican.

If Fascist Corporatism was praised as an antidote to Nazi Socialism, no objections against Hitler could be maintained once he promised to preserve the market economy, with its foundation of private property. Finally, if Hitler only was opposed for his will to total power, this political strategy against National Socialism broke down when he moved into coalition with the nationalist and conservative Right, from the German Nationalist Party to the Stahlhelm.

It is of course impossible to show precisely how strongly the Fascist precedent in Italy contributed to the readiness with which Hindenburg, the Reichswehr and the nationalist and conservative elites accepted Hitler's rise to power. However, it seems indisputable that the Italian precedent and its discussion in Germany helped to make Hitler's appointment as Reich Chancellor appear tolerable. In an indirect way, at least, the invocation of a Fascist alternative contributed to making Hitler possible. Unfortunately, after 30 January 1933 it quickly became clear that Hitler was more than 'just' a German Mussolini. Within a short time Hitler surpassed his Italian role-model. He shaped a totalitarian regime of a kind that Mussolini had tried to achieve in vain. Hitler's conservative partners on his way to power made a historical error of judgement: they trusted that Hitler would stay in the footsteps of his role-model. But Hitler only imitated Mussolini while he was on his way to power. After the seizure of power, he went his own disastrous and fatal way.

Notes

1. Cf. Ernst Nolte, 'Nationalsozialismus und Faschismus im Urteil Mussolinis und Hitlers', in *Faschismus – Nationalsozialismus. Ergebnisse und Referate der italienisch-deutschen Historikertagung in Trier*, Braunschweig 1964, 60–72; Joachim Fest, *Hitler. Eine Biographie*. Frankfurt am Main/Berlin/Wien 1964, 685–90; Jens Petersen, 'Italien in der außenpolitischen Konzeption Hitlers', in Kurt Jürgensen and Reimer Hansen (eds), *Historisch-politische Streiflichter. Geschichtliche Beiträge zur Gegenwart*, Neumünster 1971, 206–20.

2. Adolf Hitler, *Die südtiroler Frage und das deutsche Bündnissystem*, Munich 1926, 6.

3. Andreas Hillgruber (ed.), *Staatsmänner und Diplomaten bei Hitler. Vertrauliche Aufzeichnungen über Unterredungen mit Vertretern des Auslandes. 2: 1942–1944*,

Frankfurt am Main 1970, 452 (Conversation with the President of Slovakia Tiso, 12.5.1944).

4. *Hitlers Politisches Testament. Die Bormann-Diktate vom Februar und April 1945*, Hamburg 1983, 88. Cf. Frederic W. Deakin, *Die brutale Freundschaft. Hitler, Mussolini und der Untergang des italienischen Faschismus*, Cologne and Berlin 1962, 900.

5. Cf. Hans-Ulrich Thamer, *Verführung und Gewalt. Deutschland 1933–1945*, Berlin 1980, 153–9; Hans-Ulrich Thamer, 'Der Marsch auf Rom – ein Modell für die nationalsozialistische Machtergreifung', in Wolfgang Michalka (ed.), *Die nationalsozialistische Machtergreifung*. Paderborn 1984, 245–60.

6. Cf. John P. Diggins, *Mussolini and Fascism. The View from America*, Princeton/N.J. 1972; Pierre Milza, *L'Italie fasciste devant l'opinion française 1920–1940*, Paris 1967; Walter Crivellin, *Cattolici francesi e fascismo italiano.'La vie intellectuelle'* (1928–1939). Presentazione di Franceso Traniello, Milan 1984; Jerzy W. Borejsza, *Il fascismo e l'Europa orientale. Dalla progaganda all'agressione*. Rome 1981; Marco Palla, *Fascismo e Stato corporativo. Un'inchiesta della diplomazia britannica*. Milan 1991.

7. Erwin von Beckerath, *Wesen und Werden des faschistischen Staates*. Berlin 1927 (Darmstadt 1979), 154.

8. Cf. Adrian Lyttelton, *The Seizure of Power. Fascism in Italy 1919–1929*. London 1973; Renzo De Felice, *Mussolini il rivoluzionario 1883–1920*. Turin 1966; Renzo De Felice, *Mussolini il fascista I. La conquista del potere 1921–1925*. Turin 1966, Renzo De Felice, *Mussolini il fascista II. L'organizzazione dello Stato fascista 1925–1929*. Turin 1968; Renzo De Felice, *Mussolini il duce I. Gli anni del consenso 1929–1936*, Turin 1974.

9. Arthur Moeller van den Bruck, 'Italia docet', in *Gewissen*, 6.11.1922; Hans Schwarz (ed.), *Moeller van den Bruck. Das Recht der jungen Völker. Sammlung politischer Aufsätze*. Berlin 1932, 123f.

10. Cf. Fritz Sternberg, 'Illusionen über Hitler', *Die Weltbühne*, 26.8.1930; Fritz Sternberg, 'Das italienische Beispiel', *Die Weltbühne*, 17.2.1931; Rudolf Leinhard, 'Mussolinis Kriegserzählungen', *Die Weltbühne*, 26.8.1930; Rudolf Leinhard, 'Legaler Faschismus', *Die Weltbühne*, 27.1.1931.

11. Cf. Wolfgang Wippermann, *Zur Analyse des Faschismus. Die sozialistischen und kommunistischen Faschismustheorien 1921–1945*. Frankfurt am Main 1981; Barbara Timmermann, *Die Faschismus-Diskussion in der Kommunistischen Internationalen (1920–1935)*. Diss. Phil. Cologne 1977; Claudio Natoli, *La Terza Internazionale ed il fascismo 1919-1933. Proletariato di fabbrica e reazione industriale nel primo dopoguerra*. Rome 1982.

12. 'Der deutsche Faschismus', *Der Vorwärts*, 18.11.1922; 'Nein! Nein! Nein!', *Der Vorwärts*, 15.2.1933.

13. Hermann Heller, *Gesammelte Schriften*, vol. 2, Leiden 1971, 463–609.

14. Ibid. 609.

15. Ibid. 606.
16. *Der Vorwärts*, 8.2.1932.
17. I am preparing a detailed study on this topic.
18. Theodor Wolff, 'Bei Mussolini', *Berliner Tageblatt*, 11.5.1930; 'Intervista con il "Berliner Tageblatt", in Benito Mussolini, *Opera Omnia*. vol. 24, Florence 1958, 224.
19. *Frankfurter Zeitung*, 12.5.1930; Klaus Mann, 'Der Wendepunkt. Ein Lebensbereich' n.p. 1952, p. 309. Cf. Bernd Sösemann, *Das Ende der Weimarer Republik in der Kritik der demokratischen Publizisten*. *Theodor Wolff, Ernst Feder, Julius Elbau, Leopold Schwarzschild*, Berlin 1976, 139; Wolfram Köhler, *Der Chef-Redakteur. Theodor Wolff. Ein Leben in Europa 1868–1943*. Düsseldorf 1978, 225–7.
20. *Mussolinis Gespräche mit Emil Ludwig*. Berlin/Vienna/Leipzig 1932.
21. Ibid. 38, 35, 37.
22. Ibid. 131–42, 14.
23. Theodor Wolff, 'Bei Mussolini', *Berliner Tageblatt*, 11.5.1930.
24. Ibid. *Mussolinis Gespräche mit Emil Ludwig*, p.163; Theodor Wolff, 'Kommentare zu einem Gespräch', *Berliner Tageblatt*, 18.5.1930.
25. Victor Klemperer, *Leben sammeln, nicht fragen wozu und warum. Tagebücher 1925–1932*, Berlin 1996, 753.
26. Hans Reupke, *Das Wirtschaftssystem des Faschismus. Ein Experiment der Planwirtschaft auf kapitalistischer Grundlage*. Berlin 1930.
27. Ibid. 115.
28. Cf. *Verhandlungen der Stadtverordneten-Versammlung zu Köln vom Jahre 1929*, Cologne 1930, p. 6.
29. Cf. Carlo Scorza, *Fascismo idea imperiale*, Rome 1932, 65–7.
30. Heinrich Brüning, *Memoiren 1918–1934*. Stuttgart 1970, 355.
31. Cf. Edmund Freiherr Raitz von Frentz, 'Vertrauliche Informationsbriefe, 31.12.1931', quoted by Jutta Bohn, *Das Verhältnis zwischen katholischer Kirche und faschistischem Staat in Italien und die Rezeption in deutschen Zentrumskreisen (1922–1933)*. Frankfurt am Main/Berlin/Bern 1992.
32. Cf. Edmund Freiherr Raitz von Frentz, 'Hitler – Mussolini. Eine Gegenüberstellung', *Germania*, 9.4.1931; cf. Edmund Freiherr Raitz von Frentz, 'Vertrauliche Informationsbriefe, 6.6.1932', quoted by Bohn, *Das Verhältnis zwischen katholischer Kirche und faschistischem Staat in Italien*, 307.
33. Eugen Kogon, 'Wirtschaft und Diktatur. Das italienische Beispiel', *Hochland* 24 (1926), 406. Cf. Karl Prümm, *Walter Dirks und Eugen Kogon als katholische Publizisten der Weimarer Republik*. Heidelberg 1984, 101–20.
34. Anton Hilckmann, 'Fascismus und "Faschismus"', *Allgemeine Rundschau*, 2.2.1930.
35. Cf. Klaus Peter Hoepke, *Die deutsche Rechte und der italienische Faschismus. Ein Beitrag zum Selbstverständnis und zur Politik von Gruppen und Verbänden der deutschen Rechten*. Düsseldorf 1968, 307–17; Alfred Kube, *Pour le mérite*

und Hakenkreuz. Hermann Göring im Dritten Reich. München 1968, 18, 33–
6: Meir Michaelis, 'La prima missione del principe d'Assia presso
Mussolini (agosto '36)', *Nuova Rivista Storica* 55, 1971, 367–70.

36.   Letter from the crown prince to his father, the former emperor, Wilhelm
      II, of 7.5.1928, quoted by Sigurd von Ilsemann, *Der Kaiser in Holland.*
      Aufzeichnungen des letzten Flügeladjudanten Kaiser Wilhelms II, vol. 2, ed.
      Harald von Königswald. München 1968, 95.
37.   Cf. Volker Berghahn, *Der Stahlhelm. Bund der Frontsoldaten 1918–1935.*
      Düsseldorf 1966, 51.
38.   'Will Mussolini ein zweites Elsaß schaffen? Deutsches Frontsoldatentum
      und italienischer Faschismus. Unser Kampf für Südtirol', *Der Stahlhelm*,
      11.3.1923.
39.   Giuseppe Renzetti, 'Italien und Deutschland' *Der Stahlhelm*, 16.11.1930.
      Cf. on Renzetti: Hans Woller, 'Machtpolitisches Kalkül oder ideo-
      logische Affinität? Zur Frage des Verhältnisses zwischen Mussolini
      und Hitler vor 1933', in Wolfgang Benz, Klaus Buchheim and Hans
      Mommsen (eds), *Der Nationalsozialismus. Studien zur Ideologie und*
      Herrschaft, Frankfurt a.M. 1993, 42–63.
40.   Cf. BA Koblenz, Papers Renzetti, Nr. 16.
41.   Cf. BA Koblenz, Papers Renzetti, Nr. 9; Reports Renzetti of 14.4.1930,
      25.4.1930, 14.6.1930, 31.10.1930, 31.10.1930.
42.   Cf. Hoepke, *Die deutsche Rechte und der italienische Faschismus*, p. 293.
43.   Cf. Leopold Steurer, *Südtirol zwischen Rom und Berlin 1919–1939*. Vienna/
      Munich/Zürich 1980; Rudolf Lill (ed.), *Die Option der Südtiroler 1939.*
      Beiträge eines Neustifter Symposions. Bozen 1991.
44.   Cf. Karl-Egon Lönne, 'Der "Völkische Beobachter" und der italienische
      Faschismus', *QuFiAB* 51 (1971), 539–84; Meir Michaelis, 'I rapporti tra
      fascismo e nazismo e nazismo prima dell'avvento di Hitler al potere',
      RSI 85 (1973), 544–600; Jens Petersen, *Hitler – Mussolini. Die Entstehung*
      der Achse Berlin–Rom 1933–1936. Tübingen 1973, 65–8.
45.   Cf. Kurt W. Ludecke, *I knew Hitler. The Story of a Nazi who escaped the*
      Blood Purge. London 1938, 66f.; Roland V. Layton Jr., 'Kurt Ludecke and
      I Knew Hitler: An Evaluation', *CEH* 12 (1977), 372–86.; Edgar Rosen,
      'Mussolini und Deutschland 1922–1923', *VfZG* 5 (1957), 17–41; Walter
      P. Pese, 'Hitler und Italien 1920–1926', *VfZG* 3 (1955), 113–26; Alan
      Cassels, 'Mussolini and German Nationalism 1922–1925', *JModH* 35
      (1963), 137–57; Ernst Deuerlein (ed.), *Der Hitler-Putsch. Bayerische*
      Dokumente zum 8/9 November 1923, Stuttgart 1962, 543–7.
46.   Adolf Hitler, *Die südtiroler Frage und das deutsche Bündnissystem*. München
      1916, 6; Adolf Hitler, *Mein Kampf*, 70. Aufl. Munich 1933, 684–725
      ('Deutsche Bündnispolitik nach dem Krieg').
47.   Letter from Hans Frank to the Reichsleitung of the NSDAP in Munich
      of 10.8.1926, in Hoepke, *Die deutsche Rechte und der italienische Faschismus*,
      327.

48. Alfred Rosenberg, *Der Zukunftsweg der deutschen Außenpolitik*, Munich 1927, 67. Cf. Alfred Rosenberg, 'Krisenstimmung', *Völkischer Beobachter*, 9.2.1926; Alfred Rosenberg, 'Der jüdisch-freimaurische Weltkampf gegen Deutschland und Italien', *Völkischer Beobachter*, 13.2.1926.
49. Elke Fröhlich (ed.), *Die Tagebücher von Joseph Goebbels. Sämtliche Fragmente. Part I: Aufzeichnungen 1924–1941*, vols 1–4. Munich 1987, here: vol. 1, p. 259 (entry of 29.8.1928) and 436: 'Dieses italienische Kroppzeug verdient gar nicht den großen Mann' (entry of 6.10.1930)
50. Ibid. 486 (entry of 19.1.1930).
51. Hermann Göring, 'Zum deutsch-italienischen Konflikt I–III', *Völkischer Beobachter*, 3.3.1926, 6.3.19126, 9.3.1926.
52. Ibid. 9.3.1926.
53. Ibid. 3.3.1926.
54. Ibid. 6.3.1926.
55. Cf. the report of the italian press officer in Berlin, Francesco Antinori, of 18.2.1930, in *Documenti Diplomatici Italiani* Ser. 7, vol. 8, Rome 1972, 438f.; Fröhlich (ed.), *Die Tagebücher von Joseph Goebbels. Sämtliche Fragmente. Part 1: Aufzeichnungen 1924–1941*, Vol. 1–4. München 1987, here: vol. 1, p. 525 (entry of 6.4.1930).
56. Cf. Hitler's letter to Mussolini of 8.6.1933 (in Italian translation), in Renzo De Felice, *Mussolini e Hitler. I rapporti segreti 1922–1933. Con documenti inediti*. Florence 1975, p. 229.
57. Hermann Göring, 'Zum deutsch–italienischen Konflikt II', *Völkischer Beobachter*, 6.3.1926.
58. Cf. Reinhard Kühnl, *Die nationalsozialistsiche Linke 1925–1930*, Meisenheim 1966, 203–6; Hoepke, *Die deutsche Rechte und der italienische Faschismus*, 202–13.
59. Cf. Hans Reupke, *Der Nationalsozialismus und die Wirtschaft. Erläuterungen der wirtschaftlichen Programmpunkte und Ideenlehre der nationalsozialistischen Bewegung*. Berlin 1931.
60. Cf. Erich Koch, 'Sind wir Faschisten?', *Arbeitertum*, 1.7.1931.
61. Cf. Hermann Esser, 'Wucherfreiheit im Volksstaat?', in: *Völkischer Beobachter*, 8.11.1922.
62. Percy Ernst Schramm (ed.), *Dr. Henry Picker, Hitlers Tischgespräche im Führerhauptquartier 1941–1942*, Stuttgart 1963, 133f.
63. Adolf Hitler, 'Die Toten des 9. November 1923' (9.11.1927), in Bärbel Dusik (ed.), *Hitler: Reden, Schriften, Anordnungen. Februar 1925 bis Januar 1933*, Vol. 2/2, Munich/London/New York/Paris 1992, 545.
64. Hitler's speech on the occasion of the Berlin visit of Mussolini, 28.9.1937, quoted by Max Domarus (ed.), *Hitler: Reden und Proklamationen 1932–1945*, vol. 1/2, Wiesbaden 1973, 737.

NORBERT FREI

People's Community and War: Hitler's Popular Support

One of the main topics of Nazi propaganda during the Weimar Republic was the promise that in a rebuilt Germany a strong and uniform People's Community, a *Volksgemeinschaft*, would take the place of quarrelling parties, antagonistic classes and dissenting social interests. Not that it became clear how such a *Volksgemeinschaft*, which had been propagated since the Wilhelmine Empire, could be achieved and how it would be structured in detail. But somehow it took place – in the eyes of the Nazis – as part of the political 'miracle' that was their relatively effortless seizure of power. The period of terror and 'coordination' (*Gleichschaltung*) had scarcely come to an end when the *Volksgemeinschaft* had became a reality, at least from the perspective of Nazi propaganda. As the Führer himself claimed at a Stahlhelm meeting in Hanover in September 1933, 'that we won the people, that the people belong to us, that the people acknowledge our movement as the leadership, this is what matters and this is what makes us happy.'[1]

After the war, declamatory statements like this were reason enough for the newly established discipline of contemporary history to perceive the Nazi *Volksgemeinschaft* both materially and in theory as a fictitious concept. From the 1950s onwards, it was understood among historians as a fact beyond doubt that the new state of harmony in German society, which had been relentlessly propagated by the Nazi leaders and their propaganda machine, had in reality never existed. Of course, there were some very good arguments for such a historiographical position. But it was also politically useful: analysing the *Volksgemeinschaft* concept in the framework of a theory of liberal democracy was meant to put aside the question of how real the

Volksgemeinschaft really had been and rather to emphasize the islands of resistance and dissent in Nazi Germany.

During the 1950s, contemporary history, as a young discipline, had to be very careful to ensure its public acceptability by remaining as distant as possible from the collective guilt theory,[2] the main political neurosis of those years. Therefore, any questions about the *Volksgemeinschaft* could be asked only if a negative answer was guaranteed. Instead of looking at the broad public support, the enthusiasm for the Führer and the high degree of social integration, researchers placed all the emphasis upon the general climate of violence and repression and the totalitarian approach of the regime. To be sure, the latter was not of course entirely wrong, but at best it was only half the truth.

The need for its own legitimization was evident from the beginning of contemporary historiography. It diminished during the 1960s and 1970s, but it did not completely vanish. In fact, it would be truer to say that this need changed its character. The new version can be described as an attempt to work against a still widespread identification with the so-called 'good things' of Nazi rule. Despite all historical education, topics like the autobahn, the allegedly low crime rate, but also the idea of a particular solidarity within the *Volksgemeinschaft*, were still popular within substantial parts of German society. At a time when those apologetic tendencies were still pretty much alive, a historian like David Schoenbaum[3] who nevertheless decided to look at the real social basis of the *Volksgemeinschaft* ideology saw himself accused of not being sufficiently critical. In his book, *Hitler's Social Revolution*, Schoenbaum had allegedly omitted the necessary *Ideologiekritik*. As Heinrich August Winkler asked in his enthusiastic review of Tim Mason's important but in this respect rather orthodox book[4] on the German working class and the *Volksgemeinschaft*: 'What reasons are there which actually should make us accept the Nazi slogans as real?'[5]

If one puts it that way, there is, of course, no doubt about the answer. It goes without saying that historians have to break through the synthetic facade of a regime which, instead of providing the promised social benefits, led to a political and moral catastrophe of dimensions that have changed world history. The reality of everyday life in Germany during the twelve years of Nazi rule, however, cannot be correctly interpreted if one looks at it only from the perspective of the regime's monstrous end. Instead, it is necessary to look also at periods of 'normalcy' – and ask whether they were real or imagined. One must take into account collective feelings and subjective experiences which in part seemed to be more positive than was to be expected under the objective political circumstances of a dictatorship. The importance of a history of experiences has been brought to the surface during the boom of *Alltagsgeschichte* and Oral History[6] in the 1980s. Since then it became even more evident that the self-perception of German society during the Nazi period considerably affected political reality. It was interesting to see how in this respect Tim Mason has retreated from his earlier position to some extent.[7] Similarly, Werner Conze, one of the controversial founders of modern social history, made the following, clearly autobiographical, statement: 'The NS-*Volksgemeinschaft* was more than a vision imposed by the Nazis. Force alone cannot explain the determination and effort of the German people, which were key factors in the success of National Socialism (in- and outside Germany) until 1945'.[8]

In the meantime, research has overcome the narrow framework of analysis of the political system which lasted far too long because of the controversy between the so-called intentionalists and functionalists. Now, the focus is more on general domestic developments in German society under Hitler. There can be no doubt that in this context also exaggerations and misinterpretations did occur – one has only to think about the modernization theory of Rainer Zitelmann and his friends, or of Karlheinz Weißmann's controversial book.[9] On the whole, however, it seems to me that recent research did provide us with good evidence that there can be no adequate explanation of how the Nazi regime was able to perform unless one accepts its ability to produce powerful socially binding forces. This, however, brings the *Volksgemeinschaft* back into the picture as an important factor.[10]

In the following,[11] I would first like to provide you with a few impressions of how Hitler made use of the *Volksgemeinschaft* terminology and briefly to outline the ideas which he held in connection with it (I). In a second section I shall try to outline the significance of the *Volksgemeinschaft* factor during the so-called years of peace (II). My third section describes some aspects of Nazi Germany's self-perception during the war and the notion of *Volksgemeinschaft* in the face of defeat (III).

I

In Hitler's political language the term *Volksgemeinschaft* was not at all clearly defined. In fact it was borrowed from the political vocabulary of the First World War, and he sometimes used it as a mere synonym for *Volk*.[12] After the refounding of the NSDAP in 1925, he talked occasionally, and more often from 1927/8, about a *Volksgemeinschaft* in the context of his demand to overcome the 'conflict of classes' and the 'desintegration' (*Zerreißung*) of the German people. For Hitler, the 'living theory of *Volksgemeinschaft*'[13] would be the amalgamation of bourgeoisie and proletariat, i.e. the 'workers of the forehead' and the 'workers of the fist' ('Arbeiter der Stirn' and 'Arbeiter der Faust'); this was his response to a far-reaching hunger for social integration among Germans which became even stronger during the economic slump of the early 1930s.[14]

Hitler's strong and obviously appealing[15] demands for a harmonization of society are by no means to be understood as the outcome of an ideological principle and were never based upon an emancipatory or even egalitarian concept of society. On the contrary, they were derived from a rather simplistic and historically outdated idea of a rigid social order. Their genuine political motive was that Hitler perceived a consolidation of the German *Volk* as the prerequisite for racial imperialism. In this concept, there was no place at all for the individual or even the idea of individual self-fulfilment. In Hitler's own words, 'the value of people and their value for the *Volksgemeinschaft* is defined only by their way of performing the work which they have been told to do'.[16]

As can be seen from this early definition (1925), Hitler understood the intended *Volksgemeinschaft* most of all as a power machine. His often repeated belief in this *völkisch* construct was a combination of racial biology, anti-Semitism and the idea of *Lebensraum*. According to Hitler, only as a homogeneous and strong-willed *Volksgemeinschaft*, devoid of any internal conflicts and weaknesses, would Germany eventually be able to fight her enemies and to conquer the required territories. Political coordination and regimentation, the abolition of social conflicts and racial purification were for him the necessary conditions for a successful policy of expansion.

There can be no doubt that for Hitler and his close political followers the concept of *Volksgemeinschaft* was above all instrumental. However, it would be a mistake to analyse the internal politics of the regime and how they were perceived by the Germans only from the perspective of Hitler's foreign policy goals. We need to take a serious look at how the *Volksgemeinschaft* was experienced by contemporaries, and we need to evaluate critically this experience in the context of our historical knowledge.

II

A fact generally overlooked by early historical research is that soon after the brutal elimination of parties and trade unions in the spring of 1933 the Nazi regime tried rather systematically to win the support of the 'German worker'. And a fact even more difficult to accept is that before long these efforts had considerable success.[17] An important source for our understanding of this process of integration is the periodic analysis reports of the Social Democratic Party in Exile which were based on information given by confidential observers throughout the Reich[18]. In addition to these *Sopade-Berichte* there is now an edition of the internal reports of *Neu Beginnen*, a leftist socialist splinter group which had already started its observations in December 1933, half a year ahead of the Social Democrats and probably with an even less blinkered view of the situation inside Germany.[19]

The first *Neu Beginnen* report covers the pseudo-elections for the *Reichstag* on 12 November 1933 at which the NSDAP – the only party one could vote for – reached 92.2 per cent while the acclamation for Germany's retreat from the League of Nations went as high as 95.1 per cent. Hitler's leftist opponents described the situation thus:

> Because of the extraordinarily high number of votes in favour of the regime even critical foreign observers were tempted to assume that the numbers had been faked or resulted from direct force and terror. Those assumptions, however, are based on a mistaken perception of the real and profound influence fascist ideology has upon all classes of German society. ... Careful observations ... show that the results of the election in general are a true indicator of the mood of the population. Particularly in rural districts and in small villages there may have been many 'corrections'. The general result indicates an extraordinarily rapid and effective process of fascistization of society.[20]

Particularly upsetting for the socialists was the fact even before the election Hitler could dare to visit large Berlin factories such as Siemens. As a consequence of his success an 'additional increase of fascist influence had to be noted'.[21] Those observations from a perspective which was clearly anti-Nazi can leave us in no doubt: only a few months after the seizure of power effective propaganda, a slight improvement in the employment rate and some demonstrations of strength in foreign policy served as an impressive policy mix. More than terror and repression, it was those successes that made people willing to go down the road leading to 'new times'. At the very least they thought twice about taking a stand against the new developments. This was true even for those whose interests and beliefs were diametrically opposed to the regime.

The main factors in this comprehensive process of societal formation were a formerly unknown strategy of mass mobilization using all technical and organizational means available – and, in connection with that, the staging of an unprecedented 'Führer-Myth'. Ian Kershaw's studies[22] have made clear how extraordinarily important it was for the acceptance of the regime to encourage a relentless idolization of Hitler. For this charismatic system it was essential to project all successes, expectations and longings on to the Führer.

From the viewpoint of the ordinary Germans during the mid-1930s the Third Reich could well be perceived as a phase of consolidated rule.[23] For large proportions of society, including workers, the ideology of *Volksgemeinschaft* seemed to be solid and even attractive. The economic boom and the growing (though meagre) chances of consumption played a major role, but more important was the feeling that life had changed: during this period, a large majority of Germans really believed in a 'national resurrection' and in their chances of a personal career, in a heroic future, and in a better life for themselves and future generations.

A permanent social activism and an egalitarian propaganda caused, as Ian Kershaw put it,[24] 'affective integration', and it helped to ensure that the uncoupling of income and social status which was described by David Schoenbaum already thirty years ago did work.[25] In a manner that was deeply frustrating to its opponents, the regime demonstrated that people did not live by bread alone and that loyalty could be won by other means than a timely increase in basic wages.

One of the most noteworthy successes of Nazi social and societal policy was the broadening sense of social equality. Where the perception of differences in rank and status was permanently questioned, even modest signs of 'mass consumption' could qualify as indicators of a rosy future. In such an atmosphere the hopes of members of building and loan associations and aspiring car-owners[26] could, like the image of steamer trips to Salazar's Portugal, be multiplied by means of propaganda.

During the last of the pre-war years everything undoubtedly went better economically than before the seizure of power, but the official virtues praised by government still remained those of saving and consumer restraint. It was all the easier to comply when 'hard workers' could now and then 'afford a little something'. If directors and workers ate their pea soup together on so-called *Eintopfsonntage* and Goebbels turned this into a celebrity spectacle in Berlin, it was to be seen as a showpiece of Nazi 'education of the people'. The messages that these events carried were that the *Volksgemeinschaft* existed and everyone was taking part; that class distinctions were less important than 'goodwill'; and that material modesty bore witness to 'national solidarity'.

Maybe these regular simple meals also saved resources a little, but of real value for the regime was their psychological effect. They suggested a collective readiness for sacrifice which also found expression in the slogans of the Nazi Welfare Organization (*National-sozialistische Volkswohlfahrt – NSV*).[27] 'A people helping itself' was the defiantly determined motto of one of the first of countless collection drives. More important than the sums collected were, in socio-psychological terms, the millions of voluntary helpers and approximately 16 million NSV members (1942), because this mass participation could be interpreted as proof of the reality of the *Volksgemeinschaft*. Certainly it required ceaseless mobilization, but where this succeeded the *Volksgemeinschaft* was more than just a myth.

It was in the nature of the regime that the *Volksgemeinschaft* idea, parallel to the 'Führer' nimbus, was sustained by its constant actualization. Symbolic declarations of loyalty had to be permanently demanded and delivered. This was the function of the official 'Heil Hitler' greeting, but also of the frequent public events with which the party continuously forced the 'national comrades' to recognize and acknowledge anew that they belonged to the *Volksgemeinschaft*.

During the so-called 'peace years', social consciousness had been changed to some extent, snobbery and class awareness had been delegitimized, mental barriers had been put aside. All of this resulted in the production of loyalty to the regime, which in itself created a socio-psychological dynamism; its strength was very useful to Nazi ideology. Due to the widely propagated argument that performance – instead of social class and rank – should be the measure, the offer of social integration became attractive to many and in fact led to a certain egalitarianism in career chances. It was precisely young workers who responded to the Nazi slogans, and even more so since propaganda was accompanied by a policy of payment by performance after the beginning of the boom.

In the labour movement during the long period of economic depression those young workers had experienced a weakening of solidarity and reacted with a certain individualization which now became rather functional. The real benefits of such a 'modern' response to the labour market, however, could not be earned before the Adenauer era, because it was the 1950s that brought the breakthrough for a new type of performance-oriented worker who took advancement seriously and left behind the paternalistic-proletarian structures of solidarity.

Generally speaking, it was characteristic of the particular mood of the German *Volksgemeinschaft* that the regime was able to preserve this spirit for a long time even during war.

III

At first we must understand that it was precisely those enormous successes of integration which created difficulties for a regime that was preparing for war. This was because in the summer of 1939, from a socio-psychological point of view, the Germans were far from being prepared to fight. To be more exact: they hoped for the preservation of this state of fragility which they still considered to be peace. Hitler had made Germany 'big' again. He had 'freed' the Saar and the Rhineland, he had brought Austria and the Sudetenland and the Memel region 'back into the Reich', and he had forced Bohemia and Moravia under the German protectorate. The 'humiliation of Versailles' had been almost obliterated. This was why the Germans loved and honoured their Führer – not because of the risks he had taken over the last couple of years, but because of the fact that all his triumphs in foreign policy had been achieved without spilling any blood.

The massive popularity Hitler enjoyed on his fiftieth birthday was not meant for the war-driven dictator. The almost boundless enthusiasm on 20 April 1939 was in honour of 'General Bloodless'. Embedded in the stylization of the Führer as the achiever of Germany's historic destiny was the unspoken fear of a war that would destroy everything that had been achieved.

Until the very beginning of the attack against Poland public opinion in Germany wanted to believe that peace could be kept, that Providence would stay on Hitler's side. Reactions to the events of 1 September 1939 were similar, and the contrast with August 1914 could not have been sharper. Apart from reckless members of the Hitler Youth and a few fanatics, nobody rejoiced – not even party members, and the Social Democrats in Exile expressed their opinion with the title of their report: 'No war enthusiasm'.[28]

The fact that the campaign in Poland ended surprisingly fast did not really improve the German war mood; on the contrary, it nourished the hope for peace. This was the political background when the news broke on 8 November 1939 that Hitler had been the target of a massive bomb attack at the Munich Bürgerbräukeller. Johann Georg Elser's failed assassination met so perfectly the needs of Nazi propaganda that after the war there was suspicion the Gestapo itself could have set the scene. In fact Elser was alone, but of course Nazi propaganda had it that 'Brits and Jews' had been behind the murder plan and only Providence had saved Hitler's life. Those allegations were not without effect: classes of schoolchildren intoned hymns of thanksgiving, and grateful 'factory leaders' assembled their workforce for a moment of reflection. Five days after the courageous initiative of the Swabian carpenter the SS Security Service stated: 'Love for the Führer has become even stronger, and the attitude regarding the war has become more positive.'[29] Like many reports in the following weeks the message of this quotation was quite clear: war was not at all popular.

Even after the uncomplicated occupation of Denmark and the Norwegian Blitz in April 1940 optimism did not last for long. Enthusiasm on a broad scale was raised only after the triumphant campaign in the West. The occupation of Paris by German troops on 14 June 1940 and the armistice with France brought war enthusiasm to its height and Hitler to the peak of his prestige.[30]

Until then, many Germans privately had still held some political and moral concerns about the war, though this did not result in their taking action. 'After France', however, all of this scepticism and hesitation dissolved into a generally shared victors' mentality. Deeply satisfied about the erasing of the trauma of 1918, the Germans lost their doubts. The last grousers fell silent, particularly when not only raw materials for the arms industries were ruthlessly procured from the occupied territories, but also the welcome supplementary ration of Danish butter for the average consumer. Scruples about the violence with which Germany had invaded Europe seemed to be obliterated, as was any trace of a sense of injustice. From a socio-psychological point of view, at that time standards were established which must be kept in mind in order to understand the behaviour of the Germans during the second part of the war – or to be more precise: to understand the persistence of that behaviour.

Of course, there were other things that counted too. At the beginning of the war a new step had also been taken in domestic politics. After a period of relative calm which saw a decline in the number of political prisoners in the concentration camps, the anxiety of the regime increased, as did the intensity of the persecution of its opponents. There was a dramatic increase in the numbers of those who were convicted by Special Courts because of 'malicious criticism' (which quite often amounted to nothing more than the mutterings of someone in a bad mood). The ideological fight against groups and institutions which – if only passively – might challenge the regime's totalitarian claim became stronger. The conflict with the Catholic Church, for example, sharpened, and there was an increasing marginalization of the traditional conservative elites in the Wehrmacht, in the state bureaucracy and in the judicial system. Most importantly, however, a characteristic expansion of the groups perceived as enemies could be observed – a tendency which already in 1937/8 resulted in actions against so-called habitual criminals, the 'work-shy' and 'asocials'.

These were the people who now filled the concentration camps, together with Jehovah's Witnesses, gypsies and most notably Jews, who had been arrested with increasing frequency since the summer of 1938 and even more so, of course, after the pogroms of the so-called Reich Crystal Night in November 1938 when thousands of them were incarcerated.

Soon after the beginning of war the contours of a policy emerged within the SS complex which aimed at a general racial and social sanitization of the German population. Internal ministerial debates about such a policy started in 1940 when victory seemed at hand. The plan was to establish a Law on the Treatment of Community Aliens. It was intended to coordinate the actions of police and justice against persons who were perceived to be a threat to the *Volksgemeinschaft*. While the law was never passed because of institutional quarrels, political practice continued on a path of radicalization. (It must be emphasized that those who defined what could be done at any particular stage in the first place were not the Nazi politicians but the academic experts: population statisticians, labour scientists and nutritionists, anthropologists, human geneticists, physicians and the other experts of a modern industrial civilization.)

Part of this sanitization concept was the so-called 'euthanasia' programme. The systematic gassing of the mentally handicapped and mentally ill in special death clinics was the beginning of the industrialized killing – and significantly enough, Hitler backdated his authorization to 1 September 1939. Despite deceitful attempts to conceal the truth, the mass murder could not be kept secret; rumours reached the public, and protests came particularly from the churches. After a transitional pause in the summer of 1941 the killing was perpetuated virtually until the end of the war. By this point about 150,000 patients had been murdered. To some extent, the fears of older people who thought that in the end everybody could become a victim unless he was fit for work proved to be true: those 'transferred' were 'asocials', criminals, psychopaths, homosexuals, so-called 'war-hysterics', exhausted foreign workers and the bed-ridden elderly.

Despite the knowledge of individual facts, and even the awareness of their specific consequences, for a long time barely anyone was able to gain a realistic picture of politics and society as a whole. This was a characteristic result of the different levels of information and awareness which were to be found among the Germans during the war. For this, clear evidence lies in the (apart from a few hushed voices) unrecognized monstrosity of the socio- and racial-biological project which was not only oriented against 'outsiders' but also turned inwards, against the Germans themselves. Despite the aggressive-ness of the official heredity health propaganda which for years advertised alleged human inferiority, despite the forced sterilization of hundreds of thousands, of talks about 'annihilation' and the planned 'breeding of men', the average German did not realize the extent of what was happening. That is also why he did not feel himself to be personally threatened.

It was different, though, with regard to the terror against the Jews.[31] Their systematic expulsion from German public life proceeded with bureaucratic relentlessness after the atrocities of the Reich Crystal Night. Deprived of their rights as citizens, stripped of their assets, expelled from their homes and stigmatized with the yellow star, they could from the autumn of 1941 be deported in broad daylight without much public concern, not to speak of protest. Where the trains were going, barely anybody wanted to know – precisely because everybody sensed their misfortune.[32]

There were many reasons for this fateful combination of collective neglect and general inability fully to realize the political situation. Of particular importance was the fact that people did not perceive the war as a clear alternative, either being fought for more or less 'traditional' revisionist foreign policy goals or to attain the Nazi programme of *Lebensraum*. Differences and doubts melted away because of the seductiveness of military victories. The national euphoria about military successes, and later, the hope that they might return, the infatuation with propaganda, and later on the physical as well as the psychological stress of daily wartime life – all of this obscured people's judgement. The cause, however, was a permanently propagated consciousness of being part of a *Volksgemeinschaft*, which for long stretches of time became a psychological reality and which grew even more powerful during the first half of the war.

The awareness of *Volksgemeinschaft* remained stable because the war – and especially the hope for its glorious end – produced a large number of socio-political expectations. Despite, or maybe even because, any kind of concrete political programme for the time after the war was not in sight and because Hitler avoided stating final territorial goals, the 'home front' witnessed a curiously exciting sense of a new beginning. In part consciously produced, in part the result of rivalries among the minor Nazi functionaries, this atmosphere indicated a political will which, however weak, carried ideas about a post-war national socialist order.

Particularly appealing was the plan for a Social Security System for the German People (Sozialwerk des Deutschen Volkes) which was presented to the public by the German Labour Front (Deutsche Arbeitsfront, DAF) in the autumn of 1940. The project of a unified fund for the elderly and for health, together with a lot of other social-policy reforms, was announced as a result of the special wish of the Führer so 'that victory should bring every German a better life'. In reality, general benefits were not intended, as could be seen, for example, with the pension system developed by the experts in the DAF Institute of Labour Science: not everybody would receive a pension in old age, but only those 'members of the Reich who are Germans or of related blood' and who had always performed and unconditionally fulfilled their 'duty of work'.

The average member of the *Volksgemeinschaft* probably did not think about such racist-biologicist limitations in a climate steeped in anti-Semitism and social Darwinism. Maybe more than a few, however, adopted the project because of its egalitarian intentions, which DAF leader Robert Ley propagated with considerable success and at times even with an overtone of class conflict. Also important was the fact that the dark side of each social policy measure did not show immediately.[33] Finally, the hopes of many for a better future after the war were not solely founded on their expectations of a social policy but on the aspiration for a better chance of upward social mobility. Some of this had already started to take place.

For example, conscription had lowered the class barriers even for entry to the Wehrmacht. Because of its explosion-like expansion, young men from all levels of society were now able to follow officers' careers which would have been out of reach for them in former times. Similar observations could be made in other areas. The war only accelerated the speed of social dynamics and mobility which German society had witnessed during the formative years of the regime. It was changing the social structure.

At many levels, and in nearly all social groups, men and women alike were challenged in new ways. And by no means was this felt only as a burden; more often it was perceived as the opportunity for personal fulfilment and profiling. It has been rightly stated that the Nazi Party at the time it gained power was a conspicuously young movement and that the Third Reich as a whole had been a career state; this was even more true for the war years. The notoriously understaffed home front as well as the newly conquered territories offered almost endless career opportunities and fields of employment. In general, higher positions were filled by Germans who then could, if they wanted, play the role of the master race in their treatment of forced labourers or of the local people in the occupied territories.

How long and how strongly the war seemed to fulfil the personal wishes and dreams of many German *Volksgenossen* can be seen for instance in the enormous sums the building and loan associations were able to accumulate. Even in 1943 they approached civil servants and skilled labour workers with the advertising slogan: 'Save during the war – build later!' ('*Im Kriege sparen – später bauen!*'). Another of the many examples are Wehrmacht officers who as late as 1944 applied in considerable numbers to Himmler for an allocation of land in the East.

If the sheer hopelessness of the situation had not been realized for so long even by the officers, it was not only because the truth seemed to be so intolerable, but also because the war at first seemed to be so easy and victory so close. The first two or three years left the so-called home front almost untouched. How much pain, suffering and destruction the war had brought about had only dawned on the average civilian through reports of soldiers on vacation and through the weekly newsreels, but only if he was sensitive enough and really wanted to know. Although the air war had reached the Reich from the spring of 1942, the population at first did not react with general doubts about the strength of German defences. In accordance with Goebbels' propaganda, many saw the bombing as 'terror attacks', and not at all as strategically important. The damage was repaired and people went on with their lives. It was rather subconsciously that they developed the feeling of being helplessly exposed to the attacks of first the British, and then soon afterwards the American air forces. The real shock came with Stalingrad; to be more precise, with the official admission of this catastrophe at the end of January 1943.

The socio-psychological impact of Goebbels' Berlin *Sportpalast* speech on 18 February 1943, when he announced 'total war', was indeed the acknowledgement of a catastrophic defeat. As Martin Broszat has recognized,[34] for the first time there came from the top of the regime an official acknowledgement of a disastrous situation which, however, was already felt by almost everybody. Goebbels's performance, according to reports of the SD, had a 'calming effect' on the people, who without doubt had longed for a true picture of the situation.[35] The turnaround from the overly optimistic propaganda of the previous months seemed to have had an almost liberating effect.

As many SD reports show, attacking Russia in the first place had produced fear and little understanding among the population, and the rapid failure of the *Blitzkrieg* against the alleged 'colossus on clay feet' had nourished these feelings. By the autumn of 1941 the unquestioning trust in the Führer and the belief that he was in direct touch with Providence cracked a little. The Hitler-myth, however, stayed alive for a long time to come, but from then on the abilities of political and military sub-leaders were increasingly doubted, and criticism of the party did not cease.

After the failed military coup against Hitler on 20 July 1944 the regime ceased to concern itself about the welfare of its own population. Goebbels, empowered as a 'Reich Plenipotentiary for the Total War Effort', now preached a type of war socialism which awakened memories of his origins on the left wing of the party. His demands, laced with a quasi-religious flavour, for sacrifice, the fulfilment of duty and solidarity reached a peak when he lauded the air-raid damage as a basically desirable liberation from the 'ballast of civilization'.

According to Goebbels, during the bombardments the last class barriers were finally disappearing. He was right in so far as the war and its consequences – to a far greater extent than in the preceeding years of Nazi rule – had levelled a whole range of social, cultural and regional differences. But it was also true that the burdens and sufferings of war were by no means equally shared among all groups of the population. The allied air-raids were aimed primarily at the big cities, whereas, by contrast, rural areas in the interior of the Reich remained almost untouched right up to the final weeks of the war. Munition workers were subjected to a far greater pressure to perform than office and administrative employees; death came faster on the Eastern Front than in the West. And the people who suffered most of all were those who stood outside the *Volksgemeinschaft* and for this very reason could be mercilessly exploited: foreign workers, prisoners of war and concentration camp prisoners.

How sincere Goebbels' wartime socialism really was is shown by the example of German housewives who were ordered into war production and who dared to oppose the much less rigorous recruitment of women of the 'better classes'.[36] This anger is evidence for the long internalized but now vanishing appeal of the *Volksgemeinschaft* ideology in the face of imminent defeat. The *Volksgemeinschaft* did not simply dissolve but changed. More and more the chauvinist and self-righteous community became desperate and exhausted, held together not by choice but by deploring even the smallest injustice.

However, there was no collective uprising, and even during the last few weeks of war there were only some individuals and small groups who stood up against the defence fanatics. Civic sense and courage were rare, and quite often had to be paid for with one's life. There was not only angst but also apathy. After years of political engagement and of enforced performance the moment of defeat saw no revolt of the discontented, the maltreated, the politically oppressed; not even acts of revenge, but rather a waiting defined by resignation, emptiness and overwhelming exhaustion.

That does not mean, however, that people were not preparing for change. Their collective retreat from the *Volksgemeinschaft* had already been under way for quite a while, but it took place almost exclusively in people's minds. The contrast between the visible chaos of destruction and defeat and the silent collective withdrawal from the regime could not have been greater. Yet this subdued *dénouement* also expressed a hidden sense of complicity. Had not the Germans cooperated enthusiastically with the regime and all too long cheered the Führer? Many began to remember their personal opportunism and how they had accepted compromises with a greater or lesser degree of bad conscience – for instance the profiteering of the so-called 'Aryanizing' of Jewish property. And many noticed that they had not emerged unscathed from the 'great era'. Silence in the moment of defeat was not solely an expression of limitless disappointment and bitterness; it was sometimes also a sign of shame.

It is most interesting to see that in some respects only now, half a
century after the end of the Third Reich, a closer look at the German
Volksgemeinschaft experience seems to be possible. For reasons that
doubtlessly had to do with national apologia, the question of how much
and what kind of support the Nazi regime had found was – to say the
least – not welcomed in post-war Germany. It was certainly more
instinctively than consciously that even a critical historiography
avoided addressing those questions.[37]

Of course, it was – and still is – difficult to accept that more or less
a whole nation was willing to follow a dictator like Hitler and to
identify with most of his political goals, and, to a large extent even
with his policy against the Jews. In a way, the deficits of historical
research on the depth and circumstances of the *Volksgemeinschaft* are
now brought home to us in the debate about the Goldhagen book.[38]
Apart from its conceptual flaws and limitations[39] it addresses the
important question of what ordinary Germans wanted to do with those
Jews they did not want to live with any more. One does not have to
follow Goldhagen's conceptualization of 'eliminationist anti-Semitism'
to conclude: the *Volksgemeinschaft* mattered.

Notes

1. *Völkischer Beobachter*, 25.9.1933, 1.
2. See also my article 'Von deutscher Erfindungskraft oder: Die Kollektiv-
   schuldthese in der Nachkriegszeit', *Rechtshistorisches Journal* 16 (1997),
   621–34; For more about their background see my monograph, *Verg-
   ungenheit politik. Die Aufänge der Bundesrepublik und die NS-Vergabgebheit*,
   Munich 1996 (English edition in preparation: Columbia University Press,
   New York 2001).
3. David Schoenbaum, *Hitler's Social Revolution. Class and Status in Nazi
   Germany 1933–1939*, Garden City 1966 (German edition: *Hitlers braune
   Revolution*, Köln 1968).
4. Cf. Tim Mason, *Sozialpolitik im Dritten Reich. Arbeiterklasse und Volksgemeinschaft*, Opladen 1977.
5. Heinrich August Winkler, 'Vom Mythos der Volksgemeinschaft', *Archiv
   für Sozialgeschichte* 17 (1977), 484–90, quotation p. 485.
6. Cf. esp. Lutz Niethammer (ed.), *'Die Jahre weiß man nicht, wo man die heute
   hinsetzen soll'. Faschismuserfahrungen im Ruhrgebiet*. Berlin and Bonn 1983;

for a different viewpoint see Hans Mommsen, 'Einleitung', in Mommsen and Susanne Willems (eds), *Herrschaftsalltag im Dritten Reich. Studien und Texte*, Düsseldorf 1988, 9–23.

7. Tim Mason, 'Die Bändigung der Arbeiterklasse im nationalsozialistischen Deutschland. Eine Einleitung', in Carola Sachse et al., *Angst, Belohnung, Zucht und Ordnung. Herrschaftsmechanismen im Nationalsozialismus*, Opladen 1982, 11–53.

8. Werner Conze, 'Staats- und Nationalpolitik. Kontinuitätsbruch und Neubeginn', in W. Conze und M. Rainer Lepsius (eds), *Sozialgeschichte der Bundesrepublik. Beiträge zum Kontinuitätsproblem*. Stuttgart 1983, 441–67, citation p. 456.

9. Cf. from the perspective of the New Right the description by Karlheinz Weißmann, *Der Weg in den Abgrund. Deutschland unter Hitler 1933–1945*, Berlin 1995.

10. Cf. Bernd Stöver, *Volksgemeinschaft im Dritten Reich. Die Konsensbereitschaft der Deutschen aus der Sicht sozialistischer Exilberichte*, Düsseldorf 1993; stimulating analysis by an eyewitness: Sebastian Haffner, *Germany: Jekyll & Hyde, 1939: Deutschland von innen betrachtet*, Berlin 1996; From a sociological perspective, if with relatively little empirical basis, there is now: Franz Janka, *Die braune Gesellschaft. Ein Volk wird formatiert*, Stuttgart 1997.

11. Norbert Frei, 'Wie modern war der Nationalsozialismus?', *Geschichte und Gesellschaft* 19 (1993), 367–87; 'Hitlers Krieg und die Deutschen', in Norbert Frei/Hermann Kling (eds), *Der nationalsozialistische Krieg*, Frankfurt am Main 1990, 283–301.

12. Cf. Hitler, *Reden, Schriften, Anordnungen. Februar 1925 bis Januar 1933*. Vol. I: *Februar 1925–Juni 1926*, edition and commentary by Clemens Vollnhals. Vol. II: *Juli 1926–Juli 1927*, edition and commentary by Bärbel Dusik. Vol. IV/1: *Oktober 1930–Juni 1931*, edition and commentory by Constantin Goschler, Munich et al. 1992, 1994 (hereafter: Hitler, *Reden* I, II, or IV), in this case Hitler, *Reden* II/1, 238 (6.4.1927); similarly Hitler, *Reden* IV, 329f. (24.4.1931).

13. Hitler, *Reden* II/2, p. 541 (9.11.1927), also p. 690 (29.2.1928) and p. 738 (3.3.1928).

14. Cf. Martin Broszat, 'Soziale Motivation und Führer-Bindung des Nationalsozialismus', *Vierteljahrshefte für Zeitgeschichte* 18 (1970), 392–409, esp. pp. 393–8.

15. Cf. Hitler, *Reden* IV/1, 59 (5.11.1930); also 319 (19.4.1931).

16. Hitler, *Reden* I, 96f. (12.6.1925).

17. Cf. Details in Klaus Wisotzky, *Der Ruhrbergbau im Dritten Reich. Studien zur Sozialpolitik im Ruhrbergbau und zum sozialen Verhalten der Bergleute in den Jahren 1933 bis 1939*, Düsseldorf 1983; Rüdiger Hachtmann, *Industriearbeit im 'Dritten Reich'. Untersuchungen zu den Lohn- und Arbeitsbedingungen in Deutschland 1933–1945*, Göttingen 1989; Martin

Rüther, *Arbeiterschaft in Köln 1928–1945*, Köln 1990; Wolfgang Zollitsch, *Arbeiter zwischen Weltwirtschaftskrise und Nationalsozialismus. Ein Beitrag zur Sozialgeschichte der Jahre 1928 bis 1936*, Göttingen 1990; Matthias Frese, *Betriebspolitik im Dritten Reich. Deutsche Arbeitsfront, Unternehmer und Staatsbürokratie in der westdeutschen Großindustrie 1933–1939*, Paderborn 1991; summing up, Ulrich Herbert, "The Real Mystery in Germany'. The German Working Class during the Nazi Dictatorship', in Michael Burleigh (ed.), *Confronting the Nazi Past. New Debates on Modern German History*, London 1996, 23–36.

18. *Deutschland-Berichte der Sozialdemokratischen Partei Deutschlands (Sopade) 1934–1940*, Salzhausen and Frankfurt 1980 (hereafter: *Sopade-Berichte*).

19. Bernd Stöver (ed.), *Berichte über die Lage in Deutschland. Die Meldungen der Gruppe Neu Beginnen aus dem Dritten Reich 1933–1936*, Bonn 1996.

20. Ibid., p. 2; cf. Rudolf Heberle, 'Zur Soziologie der nationalsozialistischen Revolution. Notizen aus dem Jahre 1934', *Vierteljahrshefte für Zeitgeschichte* 13 (1965), 438–45.

21. Stöver, *Berichte*, 7f.

22. Cf. especially Ian Kershaw, *Der Hitler-Mythos. Volksmeinung und Propaganda im Dritten Reich*, Stuttgart 1980; id., *Hitlers Macht. Das Profil der NS-Herrschaft*, München 1992; id., 'Working towards the Führer'. Reflections on the Nature of the Hitler Dictatorship', *CEH* 2 (1993), 103–18.

23. Norbert Frei, *National Socialist Rule in Germany. The Führer State 1933–1945*. Oxford and Cambridge/Mass. 1993, esp. 70–108.

24. This is the printed formulation (as part of a generally sceptical interpretation) by Ian Kershaw, *Der NS-Staat. Geschichtsinterpretationen und Kontroversen im Überblick*. Reinbek 2nd edn 1994, 260.

25. Schoenbaum, *Braune Revolution*, esp. 150f.

26. On propaganda about the Strength through Joy car see Hans Mommsen Manfred Grieger, *Das Volkswagenwerk und seine Arbeiter im Dritten Reich*. Düsseldorf 1996, 179–202.

27. Herwart Vorländer, 'NS-Volkswohlfahrt und Winterhilfswerk des deutschen Volkes', *Vierteljahrshefte für Zeitgeschichte* 34 (1986), 341–80.

28. *Sopade-Berichte* 1939, 980.

29. Heinz Boberach (ed.), *Meldungen aus dem Reich 1938-1945. Die geheimen Lageberichte des Sicherheitsdienstes der SS*, Herrsching 1984 (hereafter: *SD-Berichte*), 449 (13.11.1939).

30. Cf. Kershaw, *Hitler-Mythos*, 136.

31. Cf. Avraham Barkai, 'The German Volksgemeinschaft from the Persecution of the Jews to the "Final Solution"', in Burleigh (ed.), *Confronting*, 84–97.

32. Cf. Ian Kershaw, *Popular Opinion and Political Dissent in the Third Reich. Bavaria 1933–1945*, Oxford 1983, pp. 358–72; Hans Rothfels (ed.), 'Zur "Umsiedlung" der Juden im Generalgouvernement', *Vierteljahrshefte für Zeitgeschichte* 7 (1959), 333–6.

33. This is true for the Law to Protect Youth of 1938 or the Mother Protection Law of 1942.

34. Martin Broszat, 'The Third Reich and the German People'. Unpublished lecture manuscript, p. 20.

35. *SD-Berichte*, 4831.

36. *SD-Berichte*, 4733.

37. Cf. My sketch: 'Farewell to the Era of Contemporaries. National Socialism and its Historical Examination en Route into History', *History & Memory* 9 (1997), 59–79. Cf. Winfried Schulze, *Deutsche Geschichtswissenschaft nach 1945*, München 1989; Peter Schöttler (ed.), *Geschichtsschreibung als Legitimationswissenschaft 1918–1945*, Frankfurt am Main 1997; Winfried Schulze/Otto Gerhard Oexle (ed.) *Deutsche Historiker im Nationalsozialismus*, Frankfurt a. M. 1999.

38. Daniel Goldhagen, *Hitlers willige Vollstrecker. Ganz gewöhnliche Deutsche und der Holocaust*, Berlin 1996.

39. The English version of my criticism from the *Süddeutsche Zeitung* of 13./14.4.1996 is printed in Robert Shandley (ed.), *Unwilling Germans? The Goldhagen Debate*, Minneapolis and London 1998, 35–9.

CHRISTOPH BUCHHEIM

The Nazi Boom: An Economic Cul-de-Sac

Looking at the following diagram one gets the impression of vigorous growth of social product per head in Germany after 1932. Unlike the Weimar Republic, the actual growth path, starting from the depth of the Great Depression, appears to be rapidly approaching the long-term trend of potential growth. The economic boom between 1932 and 1938 even seems to have been comparable to that in West Germany after the currency reform of 1948. And indeed it sometimes was also called an 'economic miracle'.[1]

Parallel to this strong Nazi upswing, unemployment was reduced, although not as quickly as official statistics might suggest.[2] But in the second half of the 1930s a situation of full employment was nearly reached – with rather big differences, however, especially regarding working hours, between industries and regions.[3] Nevertheless, after the frightening experience of extremely high unemployment during the Great Depression this fact greatly contributed to the loyalty of the German people, including the working class, towards the regime of Hitler. Even in retrospect, popular opinion is convinced that the economic policy of the National Socialist government before the war was more or less a success story.

The following chapter will show, first, that the growth achieved up to 1938/9 was of a very special nature. It deformed the structure of the German economy and already carried in itself the seed of eventual decline. Then the consequences of this for the activity of private enterprises will be explored. Finally, it is argued that an alternative to the futile Nazi Boom existed which would have produced far healthier growth with more positive effects.

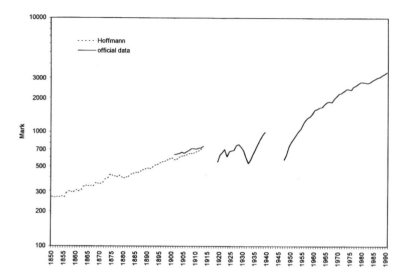

Figure 1   Social Product per Head in (West-)Germany 1850–1990 in Prices of 1913 (Mark)

Sources: W. G. Hoffmann, *Das Wachstum der deutschen Wirtschaft seit der Mitte des 19. Jahrhunderts*, Berlin 1965, 172–4, 453–5 (Germany 1850–1913); A. Ritschl/M. Spoerer, 'Das Bruttosozialprodukt in Deutschland nach den amtlichen Volkseinkommens- und Sozialproduktsstatistiken 1901–1995', *Jahrbuch für Wirtschaftsgeschichte* 1997/2, 27–54 (deflator); Statistisches Reichsamt, *Das deutsche Volkseinkommen vor und nach dem Kriege*, Berlin 1932, 32, 60, 174 (NNP: 1901–1913; 1925–1928); *Statistisches Jahrbuch für das Deutsche Reich 1941/42*, 9 (population: 1901–1937); *Statistisches Handbuch von Deutschland 1928–1944*, München 1949, 18, 600 (population: 1937–1939; NNP: 1929–1939); B. Gleitze, *Die Wirtschaftsstruktur der Sowjetzone und ihre gegenwärtigen sozial- und wirtschaftsrechtlichen Tendenzen*, Bonn 1951, 6 (NNP: 1947–1949); Statistisches Bundesamt, *Bevölkerung und Wirtschaft 1872–1972*, Stuttgart 1972, 90 (population: 1947–1959); Statistisches Bundesamt, *Volkswirtschaftliche Gesamtrechnungen. Revidierte Ergebnisse 1950 bis 1990* (=Fachserie 18, Reihe S.15), Stuttgart 1991, 46 (NNP: 1950–1988); *Statistisches Jahrbuch für die Bundesrepublik Deutschland 1996*, 47, 641 (population: 1960–1990; NNP: 1989–1990)

The Nature of Growth

As was to be expected, when the upswing accelerated, real private consumption rose by 6 per cent from 1933 to 1934. Afterwards growth continued strongly, but consumption seems to have almost stagnated, resuming slow growth only after 1936. Thus, consumption per gainfully employed person even declined by about 5 per cent between 1932 and 1938.[4] That is generally corroborated by wage statistics. Gross real hourly earnings of workers in industry increased by less than 5 per cent in the period considered, weekly earnings because of longer hours by about 20 per cent.[5] Real earnings have been calculated with reference to the official consumer price index, however, which almost certainly no longer reflected true price movements.

Thus, the Reichskreditgesellschaft estimated that the increase of the price level until 1935 was already about 20 per cent, whereas the official index rose by just 5 per cent in the same period.[6] In addition, the total of taxes and social contributions still increased over the extremely high crisis level of 1932, which had been 12.5 per cent. In 1937 it amounted to 13.5 per cent, not including the fee to the Deutsche Arbeitsfront (German Labour Front), which again was about 1.5 per cent. Moreover, there were contributions, which in practice could not be avoided, to different charities, as for example the Winterhilfswerk.[7] Therefore it seems quite clear that the real net earnings of the working population at best stagnated between 1932 and 1938. So did the average living standard, especially as there has to be taken into account the occurrence of shortages as well as the deterioration in quality of many consumer goods. By wage control, increased taxes and contributions and permission for price rises, above all for agricultural goods, the government in fact curbed private consumption, not letting it taking part in the upswing – clearly a sign of deforming growth.

But the rapid decline of the share of private consumption in the social product, the result of the policies mentioned, did not lead to a spectacular rise of the investment quota.[8] Even in the boom years 1937/8 this accounted, according to Walther G. Hoffmann, for only 14.9 per cent (net investment to net social product) and was therefore comparable to the 14.1 per cent in 1927/8, the best years of the Weimar Republic. In the pre-war period, however, it was 15.8 per cent (1911–13), and in the first half of the 1950s even 17.5 per cent. Therefore it cannot be doubted that the 'economic miracle' of the Nazi period was of a quite different kind than that after the 1948 currency reform. This was even more the case, as genuinely private investment was rather lower, because about half of the investment of industry in the years 1937/8 was brought about through the Four Year Plan and thus was initiated by the autarkic aims of Nazi economic policy.[9] Otherwise private investment was partly hindered by the monopolization of the capital market for government purposes as well as by direct investment controls.[10] But besides that there were additional reasons for the hesitation of entrepreneurs regarding new investment, as will be shown. All in all, one can state with certainty that capital accumulation was not the dynamic force in the economy in the 1930s and that high growth rates did not result from investment. Neither was that the case with real exports. In the 1920s their development was already quite weak. Only in 1929 did they almost reach their pre-war level – a reflection of the high protectionism worldwide. In the Great Depression they fell by about 50 per cent as a consequence of the shrinking of world demand and the still higher protectionism. Afterwards they hardly surpassed the very low level of 1932/3.[11] Besides external factors, strong internal causes were responsible for that. One of them was the refusal of the government to devalue the Reichsmark, leading to a highly overvalued exchange rate which constituted a heavy barrier to exports of German industry. Through several bureaucratic methods of subsidization a minimum of exports could be kept up, but not more. In this way, of course, the government had absolute control over German exports. The other internal reason for low exports was the pressure of home demand, which alone absorbed almost all the production capacities of industry. This makes it even more astonishing that private industrial investment did not grow vigorously.

Potential export possibilities improved during the 1930s compared to the crisis situation in the depression. There was even a possibility of partly liberalizing foreign trade, as the United States in 1934 had passed the Trade Agreements Act which permitted a substantial lowering of American tariffs in negotiations with trading partners. Under a different government Germany could also have profited from that. In addition, the Tripartite Agreement of 1936 between France, Great Britain and the United States showed that there was the chance to carry out unilateral devaluation without provoking immediate adverse effects. Because Germany excluded itself from such common efforts to increase the flexibility and dynamics of foreign trade, it could not raise exports substantially and thus was forced to regulate its imports even more, in order not to endanger the internal economic upswing by mounting balance of payments deficits. That resulted in not only the increasing weight of bilateralism in German trade, but also the strict rationing of imported inputs, both of which found expression in Schacht's New Plan. Again Nazi economic policy appears to have been directed against the development of a normal growth pattern.

The economic situation of the Third Reich can be interpreted as having been characterized by the overall aim of the regime – to reserve as big a share of the social product as possible for the purposes of rearmament and autarky. In doing this the government was greatly helped by the Great Depression. For in that crisis consumption as well as investment and exports fell considerably. Instead of actually having to reduce these uses of the social product in order to create room for the purposes mentioned, which would certainly have led to mounting opposition, the regime had just to restrict their growth, reserving the greatest part of the additions to the social product for itself. Thus, whereas the real social product, according to Walther G. Hoffmann, rose by an average yearly rate of about 11 per cent between 1932 and 1938, private consumption increased only by less than 4 per cent p.a., while state consumption, which included rearmament expenditures, rose by about 24 per cent p.a. Therefore the share of the latter in the social product grew quickly and in 1938 reached 26 per cent. Already in that year this was an all-time maximum for periods of peace.[12] Even today the comparable figure is lower (23 per cent in 1995).

Nothing could be less apt than characterizing the economic policy of the period as Keynesian.[13] According to Keynes, government expenditure has to replace private expenditure only so long as private forces are too weak to produce an upswing. But if they get stronger, the government voluntarily steps into the background as an agent of growth. Whereas Keynesian policy wants to stimulate multiplier effects through additional state demand, National-Socialist economic policy suppressed them as much as possible, in order to leave room for further increases of state demand. By doing so, the German economy in fact became more and more dependent for its growth on the continuous enlargement of state demand.[14]

In a basically private economy such state action, however, would eventually run up against the limits of sound financing. Of course, taxes and compulsory contributions were raised appreciably after 1932. In addition, the Reich made use of the capital market, to which it had itself secured almost sole access. But still this was not enough. Therefore the Reich resorted in increasing amounts to short-term indebtedness, the creditor being in the last instance the Reichsbank. Between 1933 and 1939 the receipts of the Reich amounted to 119 billion RM, of which about 17 per cent came from such short-term credits.[15] Thus, the amount of circulating central bank money increased, especially after 1936. In the two years until December 1938 it had grown by about half, whereas real social product rose by only 23 per cent.[16] Clearly, an inflationary potential developed in Germany which, because of the price freeze of 1936, resulted in an accumulation of surplus money from the period already before the Second World War. If this were to go on, the money surplus would finally paralyse production, as it in fact did in the period before the currency reform of 1948. The alternative would have been a severe restriction of state demand, which, however, would also have provoked a deep economic crisis, given the situation described above. In either case, the reversal of the super growth in Germany and a new depression was unavoidable and the Nazi Boom therefore is rightly characterized as an economic cul-de-sac.

The Reaction of Private Industry

The profits of industry appear to have been quite high. Table 1 gives a first impression of this fact. It shows that despite the lower price level company profits were much bigger in the late 1930s than in 1928, one of the best years of the Weimar Republic. The same applies to profits in relation to national income. Of course, interpreting the figures, one has to keep in mind that dividends were lower in the 1930s, because a law of 1934 put severe restrictions on them. But this can at most explain only a small part of the increase of retained earnings.

Table 1   Retained Profits of Joint-Stock Companies 1928, 1936 and 1938

	Billions of RM at current prices	% of national income
1928	1.3	1.7
1936	1.9	2.9
1938	3.4	4.3

Sources: *Statistisches Jahrbuch für das Deutsche Reich 1933*, 494; *1939/40*, 579

The foregoing conclusion is fully confirmed by a recent study on company profits based on tax balance sheets, which are much less prone to the creation of large hidden reserves than commercial balance sheets. Therefore they show more or less true profits. And indeed, their share in relation to the capital of firms reached

Table 2 Profits in Per Cent of the Capital of Manufacturing Joint-Stock Companies 1926–1939

1926	1927	1928	1929	1930	1931	1932	1933	1934	1935	1936	1937	1938	1939
2.24	4.17	3.32	3.31	-3.98	-7.66	-5.52	0.28	4.65	9.75	16.04	14.12	13.08	14.68

Source: M. Spoerer, *Von Scheingewinnen zum Rüstungsboom*, Stuttgart 1996, 147

maximum heights in the second half of the 1930s, as can be seen
from table 2. The average profitability of industry then was much
higher than in the 1920s. It was even higher than before the First
and after the Second World War, and it also compared very well inter-
nationally.[17] Profits, however, did not rise by the same amounts across
the board. They were biggest in those branches which were important
for rearmament, i.e. the production and investment goods industries.
Consumer goods industries, on the other hand, fared worse.
Whereas in the first group the share of profits to capital was on
average more than 11 per cent between 1933 and 1939, in the latter
group it amounted to only 7 per cent.[18]

Normally, in periods of high profits private investment is also very
high. But at this time that was not the case, as has been shown already.
Even in the producer and investment goods industries investment
proved to be rather modest. In 1938 investment was for the first time
higher than earned depreciation charges in such important sectors as
the heavy or electrotechnical industries. Investment behaviour was
only better in those branches especially favoured for autarkic reasons,
as in chemicals.[19] Therefore it was no wonder that production,
stimulated by state demand, rapidly approached the limits of capacity.
But even that situation did not make entrepreneurs more inclined to
invest and thus enlarge capacities. Instead the terms of delivery
became longer and longer, as in the machine tools industry, where
already in 1937 they were about 20 months,[20] or rationing had to be
introduced as was done in the iron and steel industry.[21]

The important question now is, why were private entrepreneurs so
hesitant towards new investment and preferred to pay back their
debts, to buy shares of other companies or simply to accumulate liquid
assets? We can discern two interrelated causes for this behaviour. The
first was just uneasiness about the strong interventionism of the state
in practically all markets, restricting ever more the room for decision-
making by firms. It is true that private ownership of the means of
production was formally preserved in the Third Reich, but the
substance of it, namely the free disposal of their uses, had been very
much limited. Thus, already in 1934 Paul Reusch demanded in the
board of the *Maschinenfabrik Esslingen* that public orders had to be
slowly diminished, in order to facilitate the spontaneous rehabilitation
of industry.[22] Later the German economy was aptly compared with
an 'espalier tree', the growth of which is very much restricted leading
to the death of one branch after the other.[23] And in 1939 Karl
Schnetzler, chairman of BBC Mannheim, said:[24]

Private initiative, which once constituted the strongest force of industry, has been restricted step by step. To be sure one wants to preserve it in principle, but for a long time one really has not been able to speak of the possibility of free economic activity. We used to find our tasks ourselves; today, however, they are given to us mostly from outside.

Even if these are only isolated quotations, they seem to reflect a widely held opinion among industrialists.

In this context exports were often mentioned as a field to which German firms had in earlier years paid special attention with good results and which in the Third Reich was almost totally strangled. This leads to the second cause of entrepreneurial caution with regard to investment, for the fact that state demand for rearmament purposes was the main propelling force of the economic upswing did not escape the attention of industrialists. But they also recognized that this could not last for ever. However, because no other dynamic forces, as for example exports, were permitted to develop, a severe economic recession could already be foreseen. Surplus capacities would re-emerge, a problem, which would greatly be aggravated if industry had previously invested heavily. In the Great Depression industrialists had recently experienced large overcapacities, and this increased their determination to avoid under all circumstances a similar situation in the future.

The foregoing analysis is confirmed by the Institut für Konjunkturforschung (Institute for Business Cycle Research) which always closely surveyed the economic situation in Germany. In 1936 it observed that the low investment could be explained by the fact 'that the high demand was a direct or indirect reflection of public ordering. It could, however, decline again if the state were to withdraw and private forces became the main elements of economic development.'[25]

To sum up so far, one can state that entrepreneurs were eager to reap the very high profits which became available during the Nazi Boom. In doing so they stretched the existing capacities of their factories to the utmost. However, in view of the cul-de-sac the boom was foreseeably running into, their economic rationality normally prevented them from greatly enlarging their capacities. Private investment in industry remained rather low. Therefore chances of long-term growth were missed. Instead of being specially conducive to growth, as the boom after 1932 might suggest at first sight, Nazi economic policy was in reality inimical to it.[26]

Table 3 Development of Costs: MAN 1927–1938

	1927	1928	1929	1930	1931	1932	1933	1934	1935	1936	1937	1938
1. Turnover (mill. RM)*	121.3	124.1	126.8	114.5	61.5	47.5	62.9	95.3	116.3	147.3	173.4	191.9
2. Total Costs (mill. RM)* [excl. material, depreciation]	64.2	66.2	65.7	53.6	34.0	26.2	34.4	46.1	58.6	69.1	80.8	91.0
3. Administrative Costs (mill. RM)		23.7	26.2	24.4	19.9	13.1	12.4	14.6	17.8	20.9	24.3	29.4
4. Wages and Salaries (mill. RM)*	40.0	41.0	42.8	34.5	20.9	15.7	21.5	29.8	37.0	42.5	48.2	56.7
5. 2./1. (%)	54.9	53.3	52.8	46.8	55.3	55.2	54.7	48.4	50.4	46.9	46.7	47.4
6. 3./1. (%)		19.1	20.7	21.3	32.4	27.6	19.7	15.3	15.3	14.2	14.0	15.3
7. 4./1. (%)	33.0	33.0	33.8	30.1	34.0	33.1	34.2	31.3	39.8	28.9	27.8	29.5

* For accounting periods lasting from July of the given year until June of the next.

Sources: MAN Archives, Augsburg: Statistiken der GHH-Konzernstelle für MAN; Haniel Archives, Duisburg: Bestand GHH 4080/35, Unkosten MAN 1928–40

Healthy Growth Was Possible – A Counterfactual Speculation

The high profits of industry were generally not, as one might think, the result of specific regulations of the National Socialist regime. Of course, wage control could be seen as an advantage, and some of the regime's measures directly contributed to the profitability of certain branches and projects, as for example privileged access to credit or contracts guaranteeing firm sales and a fixed profit margin. However, Nazi economic policy also brought many disadvantages for industry as a whole, like the rationing of inputs, the use of more expensive raw materials of German and synthetic origin, or a tax which was supposed to raise funds to subsidize exports. Thus, to explain the generally high profit potential, there must have been a widespread improvement of the cost structure of industry which occurred independently of the Nazis.

With respect to that, one has to mention the rationalization movement of the second half of the 1920s, the effects of which could not immediately be felt because of low capacity utilization, especially in the Great Depression. This crisis itself, however, contributed to far higher profits for industry as soon as it was over. This was because, first, the rationalization drive increased a lot, mainly leading to organizational improvements. Under the pressure of rapidly declining orders and production and the threat of bankruptcy, entrepreneurs did everything to cut overhead costs. And often they succeeded in doing so, even if there occurred a lag at the beginning, before the crisis displayed its really dramatic features. A fine example of this proves to be MAN, as can be seen from table 3. It shows that the share of administrative costs in turnover at first rose during the crisis, but then declined rapidly (line 6). In 1934 it reached a level about four to five points below the level before the Great Depression. So did the share of total costs (line 5). Even more importantly, however, this lower share of administrative costs could be preserved during the upswing, a fact which greatly contributed to the far greater profitability in this period. Interestingly enough, lower wages initially were not a decisive factor in this development, as the share of wage costs in turnover (line 7) despite wage control was not much reduced until 1935/6. The latter fact clearly contradicts a widely held view among historians.

A second important feature of the crisis was the reshuffling of the price structure, inasmuch as prices of manufactures and raw materials

Table 4 Shares of Value-added in Value of Production; Various Branches; per cent

	1927	1928	1929	1930	1931	1932	1933	1934	1935	1936	1937
Iron and Steel	58	61	59	62	68	73		70	69	69	70
Tyre production	43	48	45	61	65	67	65	63	60	53	
Leather industry	30	26	33	36	37	45	39	39	40	43	
Cotton spinning	26	22					42		43	41	
Margarine production		29							59	53	

Sources: Statistisches Jahrbuch für das Deutsche Reich, various issues; Vierteljahrshefte zur Statistik des Deutschen Reichs, various issues; own calculations

declined to a different degree. Whereas the former fell by about 25 per cent on average between 1928 and 1932, the latter declined by at least 35 per cent, the prices of imported raw materials alone by more than 50 per cent.[27] This meant that not only overhead costs, but also the costs of materials, measured as a percentage of turnover or the value of production, went down. The consequence was an increase of the share of value-added in the value of industrial production, as table 4 shows. Again the advantage was mostly preserved in the upswing that followed. The potential for making profits thus increased because of this fact, too. Of course, a devaluation of the Reichsmark would have reduced the extent of that increase, but probably would not have wiped it out totally. Characteristically, wages again did not play a role, as they fell, reckoned on an hourly basis, by just a litte over 20 per cent between 1929 and 1932.[28]

Therefore it can be stated that the Great Depression itself improved the cost structure of German industry quite a lot in two ways. It created a framework for far more profitable production than before. However, this remained just a possibility, as long as demand did not revive and increase capacity utilization. Precisely that, however, was effectuated in the Third Reich by the great extension of public ordering for rearmament purposes. With regard to that the question arises, whether Nazi economic policy did not in the end fulfil a vital role, in as much it provided the demand which was necessary to realize the big profit potential.

Of course, at this point the counterfactual speculation begins. However, it seems to be quite probable that, even without Hitler, the necessary demand would have come to the fore, albeit perhaps a bit more slowly. Public work creation schemes, for instance, had been started long before the Nazis came to power. The amount of funds dedicated to them had always been increasing. There is nothing to justify the assumption that this movement would have been halted suddenly if the National Socialist Government had not been installed. With regard to work creation the new regime just continued the policy of its forerunners; it behaved rather conservatively in that respect.[29]

More importantly in the longer run, however, under another government, the multiplier effects of state demand and other spontaneous forces of recovery would not have been restricted, as was done by Hitler's regime. Such forces would certainly have developed. We have seen above that private consumption in fact rose vigorously in 1934, before its further growth was artificially restricted. In 1933 the economic consolidation of other developed countries made some progress. So one could have reckoned with a rise of exports.[30] And a devaluation of the Reichsmark would have supported such a development very much, as would the participation of Germany in the activities for institutional reform of the world trading system mentioned above.

Thus, there almost certainly would have been enough demand to restart growth after 1932. Capacity utilization would have increased and profitability would soon have been achieved, given the higher profit potential after the crisis. An advantage compared to the actual situation would have been the non-discriminatory nature of the ensuing upswing. Thus, consumer goods industries in particular would have achieved higher production and profits, not being hit so much by restrictions of their purchases of raw materials and of the demand for their products. This quite large subsector of industry, therefore, would have contributed far more to further growth than it actually did. Finally, it seems quite certain that with rising profits in the more liberal economic framework described there would have been an investment boom. The basis would have been created for successful growth, catching up the long-term trend and leading to an increase of the living standards of the population, as was in fact the case after 1948.

As it was, Nazi economic policy, effected in an economy characterized by private ownership of the means of production, was necessarily leading into a cul-de-sac with a new crisis to come. This fact alone prevents us, of course, from applauding that policy, as is sometimes still done. If it had been the sole way out of the very high unemployment of the crisis years, one could still discuss its economic merits. But, if the scenario outlined above seems at least plausible, the conditions of the time were different. There was an alternative way out of the crisis which would have led to healthy growth and an improvement of living standards, an improvement which, however, was not realized, precisely because the National Socialist regime actively prevented it. Seen from that angle, Nazi economic policy was a catastrophe. It prolonged the sickness of the German economy, which Knut Borchardt attested the Weimar Republic,[31] for a further fifteen years. And in a way it made the war seem capable of providing a solution to the economic problems which were to come. First, the discipline necessitated by it probably enlarged the possibility of accumulating a money surplus without devastating effects on production. Secondly, it allowed speculation that after a German victory the countries which would have lost the war could be made to pay its costs, thus providing the material resources to cover the surplus money.

Notes

1. H. Priester, *Das deutsche Wirtschaftswunder*, Amsterdam 1936.
2. C. Buchheim, 'Zur Natur des Wirtschaftsaufschwungs in der NS-Zeit', in C. Buchheim, M. Hutter and H. James (eds), *Zerrissene Zwischenkriegszeit. Wirtschaftshistorische Beiträge. Knut Borchardt zum 65. Geburtstag*, Baden-Baden 1994, 102–7.
3. R. Hachtmann, 'Arbeitsmarkt und Arbeitszeit in der deutschen Industrie 1929 bis 1939', *Archiv für Sozialgeschichte* 27, 1987, 187–92.
4. W. G. Hoffmann, *Das Wachstum der deutschen Wirtschaft seit der Mitte des 19. Jahrhunderts*, Berlin 1965, 174, 206, 826, 828.
5. *Statistisches Jahrbuch für die Bundesrepublik Deutschland 1990*, 502, 548.
6. L. Grebler, 'Die deutsche Arbeitsbeschaffung 1932–1935', *Internationale Rundschau der Arbeit* 15 (1937), 828–9.
7. 'Die Entwicklung der Arbeitsverdienste in den letzten zehn Jahren', *Wirtschaft und Statistik* (1938), 158–61.
8. This is confirmed by A. Ritschl, 'Die NS-Wirtschaftsideologie – Modernisierungsprogramm oder reaktionäre Utopie?', in M. Prinz and R. Zitelmann (eds), *Nationalsozialismus und Modernisierung*, Darmstadt 1991, 50–1. The contrary, however, is stated by Overy; see R. J. Overy, *The Nazi Economic Recovery 1932–1938*, London 1982, 35–41.
9. Hoffmann, *Wachstum*, 247, 826; D. Petzina, *Autarkiepolitik im Dritten Reich. Der nationalsozialistische Vierjahresplan*, Stuttgart 1968, 183.
10. S. Lurie, *Private Investment in a Controlled Economy. Germany, 1933–1939*, New York 1947, 100–11; 200–11
11. Hoffmann, *Wachstum*, 531.
12. Ibid., 826, 828.
13. For more details compare R. Erbe, *Die nationalsozialistische Wirtschaftspolitik 1933–1939 im Lichte der modernen Theorie*, Zürich 1958.
14. Similarly H. James, *The German Slump. Politics and Economics 1924–1936*, Oxford 1986, 417–8.
15. F. Federau, *Der Zweite Weltkrieg. Seine Finanzierung in Deutschland*, Tübingen 1962, 20; see also Deutsche Bundesbank (ed.), *Deutsches Geld- und Bankwesen in Zahlen 1876–1975*, Frankfurt am Main 1976, 313.
16. Deutsche Bundesbank (ed.), *Geld- und Bankwesen*, 4; Hoffmann, *Wachstum*, 828.
17. M. Spoerer, *Von Scheingewinnen zum Rüstungsboom. Die Eigenkapitalrentabilität der deutschen Industrieaktiengesellschaften 1925–1941*, Stuttgart 1996, 160–1.

18. Ibid., 155.

19. *Statistisches Jahrbuch für das Deutsche Reich 1938*, 566; *1940/41*, 612.

20. T. Siegel/T. von Freyberg, *Industrielle Rationalisierung unter dem National-sozialismus*, Frankfurt/M. 1991, 165; see also A. Gehrig, *Nationalsozialistische Rüstungspolitik und unternehmerischer Entscheidungsspielraum. Vergleichende Fallstudien zur württembergischen Maschinenbauindustrie*, München 1996, 88–113.

21. Siegel/Freyberg, *Rationalisierung*, 174; J. S. Geer, *Der Markt der geschlossenen Nachfrage. Eine morphologische Studie über die Eisenkontingentierung in Deutschland 1937–1945*, Berlin 1961.

22. Buchheim, 'Wirtschaftsaufschwung in der NS-Zeit', 110.

23. H. James, 'Die Deutsche Bank und die Diktatur 1933–1945', in L. Gall, G. D. Feldmann, H. James, C.-H. Holtfrerich and H. E. Büschgen, *Die Deutsche Bank 1870–1995*, München 1995, 333.

24. Quoted by R. Peter, *Rüstungspolitik in Baden. Kriegswirtschaft und Arbeitseinsatz in einer Grenzregion im Zweiten Weltkrieg*, München 1995, 63.

25. 'Allgemeiner Konjunkturdienst. Die Wirtschaftslage in Deutschland', *Vierteljahrshefte zur Konjunkturforschung* 11, 1936, Part A, N.F., 64.

26. Ritschl, 'Wirtschaftsideologie', 59, also speaks of great possibilities for growth which remained unused in the period.

27. Institut für Konjunkturforschung, *Konjunkturstatistisches Handbuch 1936*, Berlin 1935, 101, 104.

28. *Statistisches Jahrbuch für die Bundesrepublik Deutschland 1990*, 502.

29. Compare for this H. James, 'Innovation and Conservatism in Economic Recovery: The Alleged 'Nazi Recovery' of the 1930s', in W. R. Garside (ed.), *Capitalism in Crisis. International Responses to the Great Depression*, London 1993, 71–81.

30. Institut für Konjukturforschung, *Wochenbericht 1933*, 81–2; 133.

31. K. Borchardt, 'Constraints and Room for Manoeuvre in the Great Depression of the Early Thirties: Towards a Revision of the Received Historical Picture', in K. Borchardt, *Perspectives on Modern German Economic History and Policy*, Cambridge 1991, 152–60.

ULRICH HERBERT

Ideological Legitimization and Political Practice of the Leadership of the National Socialist Secret Police

Translated from the German by Maike Bohn

At the beginning of the Second World War the leadership of the *Reichssicherheitshauptamt* (Imperial Department of Security) consisted of approximately 300 men: heads of offices, of departments, of regional police stations and their deputies. This fairly small pool of people provided a large proportion of the leaders of task forces, heads of operations, chiefs of staff, commanding officers and commanders of the Security Police (*Sicherheitspolizei*) and the Security Service, SD (*Sicherheitsdienst*), in the occupied territories as well as regional Gestapo leaders. They were directly connected with and responsible for almost all deportations, eliminations and exterminations in Germany and the occupied territories, particularly Eastern Europe. If there was ever a central group responsible for the National Socialist policies of genocide and prosecution, it was made up of these men.

It was certainly a remarkable group and very distinct from other functional elites in the Third Reich: in 1939 two thirds of these men (in the Gestapo and SD) were aged 36 and less. Almost as many had been to university, mostly studying law. Evidently, these men were neither socially uprooted desperadoes who compensated for their lack of social relations and integrity with bloodlust and murder, nor were they simply obeying orders without conviction and unaware of the consequences of their actions. If this holds true, their personalities

and convictions, their political socialization and ideological found-
ations need to become the focus of inquiry.

The combination of gifted young lawyers and the fanatical SS
ideologues and planners of mass-extinction in the leadership of Secret
Police and SD poses a political and moral challenge. The classic
patterns and expectations regarding the leaders of the National
Socialist terror do not apply here, and this provokes interpretations
of split personality, as in the case of the judges of the Nuremberg
Trial. However, this combination of radicalism, ideology and a specific
form of reason – on the one hand an internal, ideological rationality,
on the other hand an 'objectivity' (*Sachlichkeit*) combining efficiency
and functionality with ideological premises – needs to be explained
both historically and individually if we want to understand why in
the 1930s and 1940s a substantial part of Germany's young intel-
ligentsia was able and willing to conceptualize and carry out a policy
of extermination of hitherto unknown dimensions.

Furthermore, if the leaders of the National Socialist police were
neither technocratic murderers nor socially marginal recipients of
orders but intelligent, self-confident, energetic and young members
of the middle and upper middle classes of German society with their
own political views, we have to look much more closely at the society
which produced this elite. The questions raised here relate not only
to an understanding of the NS-regime or its apparatus of terror, but
to the whole of German history in the twentieth century. Hence the
issue of political and social succession gains a new dimension and
actuality that are lost by generalizing statements blaming the
Germans *in cumulo* for the murder of the Jews.

So far there has been no systematic political, intellectual, social or
biographical analysis of this leading group of the National Socialist
terror; the reasons for this can be found in the way research into the
history of the NS-regime has evolved and are therefore part of the
problem.

From the post-war period to the 1960s, police, SD and SS had
attracted considerable interest, not least because of the trials at
Nuremberg, Jerusalem and Frankfurt. The first half of the 60s
witnessed the debate about Eichmann and the 'banality of evil' in
the wake of Hannah Arendt's writing. This was no surprise in the
light of the revelations of the Jerusalem trial; Eichmann's personality
and behaviour contradicted all expectations that such a direct
participation in the biggest mass crimes in history had to correspond,
although in reverse, with a diabolical perpetrator. Eichmann turned

out to be a fanatical and small-minded organizer without personal or intellectual stature and this must have been a grotesque realization for the survivors and their families. Most probably this had a fatal effect on historiography: from now on, the zealous Eichmann who carried out orders became the role model for the National Socialist 'desk-bound perpetrator' (*Schreibtischtäter*).

However, since the late 1960s the above-mentioned group was notably absent from the growing and increasingly politicized debates. In brief, two developments emerged:

–   on the one hand, the significance of the National Socialist apparatus of terror and its organizers receded into the background as people doubted its political independence within the regime. They questioned the relevance of the world views of its protagonists for the NS state's policy of genocide and concentrated on the dynamics of structural elements of the NS system. Based on Aronson's, Buchheim's and Höhne's evaluations of the leadership of Gestapo and SD but also independently of them, an image of a cold 'technician of power' emerged; a 'technocrat of terror'; an opportunist and careerist without political convictions, merely fascinated by pure power.

–   on the other hand, the open concept, represented by Bracher in particular, was overshadowed by the intensifying political-historical debates in the late 1960s. Previous debates had underlined the dispersal of *völkisch* and racist doctrines among significant numbers of the intelligent youth of the Weimar Republic as well as the links with the elitist thought and assertions of *Volkstum* propagated by the Gestapo and SA leadership, which often differed widely from the positions of the SA and the party. To contradict the dictum of the 'weak dictator' and the implicit demand to analyse the role of the social elites during the NS dictatorship, these debates were restricted'Hitler's *Weltanschauung*, that had inevitably led to 'Hitler's rule' and the National Socialist mass crimes. It was argued that Hitler had been the only person driven by the vision of a Jewish genocide since the early 1920s and had been consistently implementing it. This interpretation does not see the leaders of Gestapo and SD as acting independently but regards them as Hitler's subordinate helpers implementing his orders. The ideological legitimation, world view and policies of race and nation of this group were seen as derived from Hitler's vision and therefore not subject to independent

research. Simultaneously, *völkisch*, social Darwinist and racist anti-
Semitic ideas were regarded as marginal and obscure, the leaders
of Gestapo and SD as exponents of a relatively small group of
fanatics with psychopathological motives and drives. As a result
'the SS' became a residual category of the abnormal and not
directly connected to the rest of society.

Thus these two interpretations do not treat the RSHA leaders as
independent agents worthy of analysis but as driven, empty instruments of power. Their actions were seen either as radical reflections
– motivated by the system or by opportunism – of existing conflicts
or deficits, or as the mere executors of the Führer's will.

The use of the term 'generation' as a historical category is prob-
lematic in so far as we cannot exactly define its boundaries nor
describe the effects of collective experience precisely and separated
from other factors. These problems seem to surface whenever we try
to use 'generation' as a general category for the entire historical
process. The concept becomes more useful if we apply it only to
specific events and developments that have a lasting effect on a
contemporary age group and distinguish it from the experiences of
other age groups – 'generation' becoming a historical factor. This is
most probably true for the First World War where individuals and
experiences were confronted with an array of meanings that linked
individual experiences to the categories and values of their 'political
generation'.

Already the political theory of generations (*Generationenlehre*),
influential in the late Weimar Republic, considered those born
between 1902 and 1912, the so-called 'generation of war youth'
(*Kriegsjugendgeneration*), as the politically most important group of
Weimar youth. It was characterized by having been socialized during
the political troubles of the post-war period. On the one hand, this
had resulted in a political radicalization, on the other in the total
rejection of the 'degenerate' and outdated culture of Wilhelmine
society. The same theory acknowledged that this generation had also
turned away from the political style of the generation of youths at
the front (*junge Frontgeneration*), born between 1890 and 1900, which
was considered too naïve and idealistic, too sentimental and unrealistic. The bourgeois youth developed a generational lifestyle that was
cold, hard and 'objective' – in stark contrast to the emotional and
personal group of their elders – and that was rooted in an all-
embracing ideological system of radical *völkisch* nationalism.

It is crucial to understand the extreme political Right after the First World War as a complex and fragmented 'movement', more often characterized by people than by clear programmatic differences, but which still saw itself as a united 'camp' consisting of multiple informal contacts and memberships as particularly seen in the conservative 'Ring'-movement. It is misleading to contrast along clearly defined lines of demarcation the intellectual groups that were united, not without intent, under the heading 'conservative revolution' after the Second World War with the *Deutschvölkischen*, National Socialist or other extremist national groups. Rather, the boundaries were fluid and people changed their adherence to one or several groupings as often as the groups themselves were founded and refounded, during the first half of the Weimar period in particular. Ernst Jünger's dictum, that of the numerous groups of the national camp the *Münchner Richtung* (the 'most superficial and plebeian' one) asserted itself, illuminates this context.

The shared political concepts of the radical Right of the Weimar Republic have been much described. They can be summed up as the rejection of 1789 and 1848 and described as anti-international, anti-liberal and anti-Semitic, with varying degrees of importance among the individual groups. In this context National Socialism was one of many movements and did not differ from them by virtue of a specific ideology but by its emphasis on organization, mass propaganda and activism instead of ideas, elites and debates. The ideological concepts of the National Socialists were eclectic and, like those of the other radicals of the Right, unoriginal. However, this is neither an argument against their effectiveness nor is it a sign of modern ideological concepts of a large scale. It helps an understanding of the process described here to interpret the development of ideological right-wing radicalism in Germany between the 1880s and 1920s as a slow evolution and consolidation rather than as a well-rounded and original philosophy.

A closer look at the political experiences of this generational group of bourgeois youth reveals three points:

1. Between 1919 and 1923 the *Völkisch-Radikalen* of the academic youth in Germany were overwhelmingly successful. The results of the AStA (General Council of Students) elections showed (with an electoral participation of appr. 70 per cent) that in spring 1921 at the latest the *Völkisch-Radikalen* – which in the context of the strong controversies about Jewish membership of German

universities meant radical anti-Semites – dominated the universities. In terms of the political theory of generations this means that the replacement of those born by about 1900 (the generation of the front youth) by the generation of the war youth (*Kriegsjugendgeneration*) accelerated the process of political radicalization.

2. This generation had grown up during the war but was formed by the turbulent post-war years. The ideological concepts of the Right had been widely spread among bourgeois youth before and during the war by the All-German and Patriotic Parties (*Alldeutsche* and *Vaterlandspartei*). However, the experience of 1917/18 and 1923 gave these concepts an empirical validation in the eyes of that youth. The occupation of the Rhineland and the Ruhr, the conditions of the Treaty of Versailles, the Spartakus revolt and separatist coups, the Polish invasions of East Germany and the oppression of German minorities in the newly created states of Eastern Central Europe, all seemed to confirm the statements of the *völkisch* Right, not the categories of human rights and democracies as declared by the American President Wilson.

3. In the long term this *völkisch*-radical youth movement of the early Weimar years which spread among that generation linked the political view of the development in post-war Germany to an ideologically defined world view and at the same time turned it into the exclusive experience of one generation. Thus *völkisch* radicalism, the rejection of the republic and democracy and above all biologically motivated anti-Semitism appeared not as one political opinion among many, but as part of a way of life, a generational style that distinguished the individual person from his liberal or democratic environment through his *Weltanschauung* and from older 'national' or conservative thinkers through radicalism, toughness, objectivity, coldness and, above all, willingness to act.

The leaders of Gestapo, SD and later the RSHA were not technocrats or subordinates fascinated by sheer power. They were young and very young men who had always thought and acted within the categories of *völkisch* radicalism and whose experiences were subsumed under their political convictions, linked into a generational style developed from this, and whose elitist understanding culminated in the courage, unlike their contemporaries, to put these insights into practice without compromise.

A brief outline of the ideological vision that dominated the leadership of Gestapo and SD can be based on two assumptions:

1. social developments can to a large extent be deduced from biological and genetic, not social constellations.
2. Peoples, not individual persons or classes, are the subjects of history. They regenerate themselves through individual subjects and receive their different abilities and characteristics through tradition and genetic code.

According to this vision the German people is particularly valuable, but its *völkisch* substance is endangered by two developments: first from within, as the modern civilizing process has protected the weak, degenerate elements within the German people. Without natural selection and as a result of this process, these elements have been able to reproduce disproportionately. As the First World War has claimed the deaths of large numbers of those with superior heritage, the number of inferior people (*Minderwertige*) has risen excessively. This view explained the various deviations from the social norm with biology, i.e. with the genetic – 'blood-based' (*blutlich*) – structure of the individual. To get rid of the worrying symptoms of modernity, from urban criminality via mental illness to asocial behaviour, people had to remove the carriers of genes containing those behaviour patterns from their national body (*Volkskörper*) and prevent them from affecting the genetic heritage of the German people.

The second danger comes from the outside – from the interbreeding of the German people with other, biologically inferior, people or races; here the term 'race' translates as 'biologically determined potential for development'. This causes severe damage to the collective genetic heritage of the people. Jewry poses the largest threat for three reasons: (a) the Jews are biologically and historically (as a people without land or state and in need of assimilation) equipped with bad genes; (b) they already have deeply penetrated the German people and its genetic substance; and (c) Jewry is the basis for political inter-nationalism of any kind all over Europe, which means opposition to the *völkisch* and national assertion of the Germans and also the basis for criminality and degeneration in the countries on the continent and even of the world.

Both developments – inner and outer danger to the German people – are seen as relatively advanced by this theory. The internal and external situation of the German people since 1918 demonstrates the ensuing inner decline and outward powerlessness. If the German people wants to deal with internal problems and secure its well-deserved leading place in Europe and the world, it has to eliminate the degenerate elements within as well as the intrusive elements of that extraneous, parasitic and degenerate people, the Jews.

These ideological concepts outlined briefly above met the irritating symptoms of modern industrial society with scientific, biological explanations. This resulted in the view that state support could help along 'natural elimination' so that the unnatural development of the past decades and centuries could be halted and reversed to create a biologically 'clean' society (almost) free of conflict. The young generation, academics in particular, took to this vision for four reasons:

1. It seemed to conform with 'progress' and 'modern developments' in science and technology and was using very 'modern' methods itself, for example the precursors of genetic research.
2. It went hand in hand with the propagation of the modern and progressive methods of a social policy that supported the 'biologically valuable'.
3. This concept did not demand any personal emotional engagement – on the contrary, it suggested objective action, detached from individual interest, hatred or lust for revenge.
4. The individual had the impression of participating actively in a project addressing the political-biological 'recovery' of the German people and, in perspective, of the whole continent to a hitherto unknown extent. People sensed the historical magnitude and 'uniqueness' of the project and were grateful to be able to contribute to this.

The precondition for all of this was to abandon the postulates of human equality and of the protection of the weak either in the tradition of Humanism or of Christianity. From the point of view of intellectual history, it was central to this process readily to regard society or the 'people' as biologically structured, 'organic' system that was organized along 'natural' principles not human ones. The *Weltanschauung* functioned as an empirically valid and tested explanatory system that was able to reconcile all contradictions. This is not a specific characteristic of the ideas discussed here; modern *weltanschaulich* dictatorships are carried by people – especially the elitist inner circle of the well-informed and clear-thinking – who regard their world view as the best means to recognize the 'essential' (*Eigentliche*) and who base their claim to leadership on this.

It is also in this context that we have to understand the various attempts by right-wing intellectuals to sever the ties with international law, to replace them with an implementation of national interest regardless of moral and legal implications, and to propagate this as being legitimate. Three elements were linked in this way of thinking: (1) *völkisch*, philosophical (*lebensphilosophisch*) and social Darwinist ideas; (2) the generational ideal of objectivity (*Sachlichkeit*) and heroism; and (3) the postulates of Carl Schmitt that were aimed against Western ideals of human and international law. On this basis people elevated the enforcement of national interest to a given, constant factor of natural law, not subject to any other rules. This natural-law concept of *Völkerrecht* rejected any attempt to formulate general human goals such as human rights, peace or general welfare. Rather, the relationships between states and 'peoples' were characterized by interests only and by the power to assert these interests. This outlook legitimized in its most radical form the total annihilation of the opponent:

> We can honour whom we have to fight or even to kill. And we begin to wish that all people who have come to this conclusion will find themselves in a chivalrous state of objectivity to simplify the daily life of people and, in their tragic decisions, to preserve their fateful dignity against the hatred and meanness with which the poorer souls try to understand and to fight incomprehensible strokes of fate. (Best: 1930)

The resulting ethics of the 'fighter' consequently denies all moral ties and is legitimized solely by the interests of his people. The fight to the death as an expression of nature and the laws of life also implied that personal feelings of hatred against the enemy were negligible, even illigitimate. The ideal was to accept and honour the enemy, who was to be fought and killed, as a fighter for the interests of his own people. In 1930, the concept of 'Heroic Realism' (*Heroischer Realismus*) became the key term to understand the thoughts and actions of the young academic Right of the Weimar years. To fight or kill the opponent without hatred but in line with natural laws and the interests of one's people meant that the fight became an 'objective task' (*sachliche Arbeit*) that was detached from emotion and passion – this idea carried the synthesis of the political concepts of 'conservative revolution' and 'military nationalism' (*soldatischer Nationalismus*) to an extreme.

National Socialism did not differ from the many other nationalistic movements by virtue of its specific ideology but because it preferred organization, mass propaganda and action over theories, elites and debates. This was seen as a deficiency by the right-wing intellectuals of the 'conservative revolution' who wanted to call the NSDAP the 'department of popular movement' (*Referat Volksbewegung*) of the national revolution. Most reservations were dropped, however, when in the early 1930s the National Socialists asserted themselves and clearly demonstrated their superiority, and when it also became obvious that the party did have a political and intellectual leadership.

The fact that many of those leaders found their place in the emerging powerful conglomerate of Himmler and Heydrich is also a typical development: there they found a sphere of action that allowed them to implement the ideas of *weltanschaulich* radicalism, 'objectivity' and elitist leadership while helping their own careers.

An important step in relation to this was the series of murders of SA leaders in July 1934. The leaders of Gestapo and SD above all, whose average age at the time was no more than 30, developed the esprit de corps and detachment from the traditional values of Western Christian education that later became so characteristic of that group.

From 1936, the leadership of the *Sicherheitspolizei* became an increasingly independent and important factor in the politics of the regime. The legal, political and organizational takeover of the entire police by Reichsführer SS as well as the merging of the criminal investigation department (*Kriminalpolizei*) and Gestapo in the *Sicherheitspolizei* in 1936 marked the transition from fighting political enemies to a general, preventive and biological concept of the police as 'doctor of the body of the German people'. The activities of the police were widened to include a 'medical' social programme to fight the socially and biologically undesirable. This became manifest in the National Socialist concentration camps after 1936/7 where 'political' prisoners became a minority compared to the 'asocial', 'professional criminals' and 'work-shy' who were interned for reasons of 'social health'. On the one hand, this can be seen as the radical conclusion of the '*völkisch*-organic' world view, on the other hand, it represents a qualitatively and quantitatively new dimension of politics and policing. This was without historical precedent and aimed at a social utopia that was free of conflict as it had isolated the carriers of socially 'damaging' genes, excluded them from procreation and finally 'eradicated' them.

In the years leading up to the war Heydrich and those close to him took great care to select young recruits for the executive of *Sicherheitspolizei* and Gestapo according to political as well as professional criteria. Relatively quickly they formed a fairly homogeneous generational, social and political leadership that was much younger than the elites in administration, economy and the armed forces and more qualified than those of the party. To a great extent they belonged to the 'political generation' of the war youth, i.e. those born between 1902 and 1912. The recruitment and training of this young elite, which was to provide the central group to plan and execute National Socialist mass murder in Europe after the outbreak of the Second World War, proved to be momentous and significant. The political socialization of the members of this group ran parallel and, moreover, the unifying world view homogenized their experiences – a necessary precondition. These political convictions proved particularly explosive in relation to the Jews. In 1932, the long-standing organizer, lawyer and ideologue of the Gestapo, Werner Best, had already formulated in the jargon of the Heroic Realism that

we simply recognize that certain people and characteristics damage our nation and threaten its existence, and we will resist this. Similarly, in the fight against the Jews our goal is freedom from domination, a clear separation and specific rights for the foreigners . . . It is irrelevant to us whether a heavenly judge will deem Jewry valuable or worthless; anti-Semitism is not a world view but a political, economic and cultural defence. The *völkisch* principle of recognition for each people and its right of existence applies equally to the relationship with all other nations. In times of conflict we will of course pursue the vital interests of our people even to the extent of annihilating the opponent – but without the hatred and contempt of any value judgement.

Two things are important here: first, this view originated from a specific concept of history and the 'rules of life' (*Lebensgesetze*) – by the way, a parallel imitation of the Marxist notion of the laws governing the historical process. This world view gained particular importance because it explained the German defeat in the First World War, cast it in the context of a conspiracy and legitimized its revenge.

This way of thinking replaced the individual with the 'people' as the central category of reference. The 'objective' interests of the German people were defined as absolute and without any higher authority; neither human rights that referred to the individual, a governing system of diverging interest such as international law nor a fixed normative structure like Christianity. As a precondition the postulates of human equality and the protection of the weak, either in the tradition of humanism or of Christianity, had been abandoned. A central factor of this process was the readiness to regard society, the *Volk*, as a biological and 'organic' structure that was organized not on human but on 'natural' principles and whose importance was as a whole, not the sum of its human parts.

Secondly, the relationship with the Jews had been stripped, whether on the surface or for real, of any individual emotions. Representatives or embodiments of internationalism, the Jews were perceived as the opposite of a Germanness fighting for national greatness. The persecution of Jews out of hatred was regarded as plebeian, immature and vulgar anti-Semitism whose expression was the pogrom and had to be overcome. Rather, the Jew had to be fought without hatred. The fight against the Jews was an expression of the interests of the German people – its proponents were often unaware of being 'anti-Semitic'.

From 1935 the leadership of SD and Gestapo developed a policy aimed at the total expulsion of Jews from Germany which was based on these assumptions and much discussed in the SD at that time. From 1938/9 this policy started to become a reality; initially in Germany and then in Poland where it turned into the gigantic programme of resettlement and deportation whose failure resulted in the planned mass murder of the Jews.

At the beginning of the war at the latest, the maxims of Heroic Realism became extremely relevant for the leadership of *Sicherheitspolizei* and Gestapo: the *weltanschaulich* fighter was stylized as executor of the interests of the people and as someone who had no values or laws beyond these but felt no personal hostility towards the opponent even when killing him. At that time, these unrealistic postulates became the legitimation for the leaders of the task forces (*Einsatzkommandos*) and the organizers of mass deportations, who had grown up with the ideas of toughness and 'objectivity' and were now put to the test.

The doctor who chose the 'mentally deficient' for the next deathly transport; the charity worker who discovered an 'asocial clan' (*asoziale Sippe*); the demographer who postulated the supposed 'overpopulation' of half of the continent and suggested the depopulation of entire regions; as well as the head of department at the RSHA who ordered the deportation and ghettoization of the Jews or the head of operations who ordered the execution of the Jewish population of a district in Ukraine – all of them were able to understand and legitimize their actions as expression of an 'objectively' necessary and 'natural' concept of 'biological cleansing of the German national body' and of '*völkisch*' reallocation of the land in Europe. People related their actions to these views, which not only protected them from intervention but also took away their inhibitions and exonerated them. Their actions were justified by declaring them as necessary means to a higher goal that remained unquestioned and thus repudiated the humanitarian principles they had been brought up with.

Now it became obvious that the *weltanschaulich* charge on the one hand, and the lack of consistency and of values attached to the ideological doctrine on the other, were closely linked to the symbolic intensification of a conviction into an 'attitude', a 'mentality' that allowed the individual to do the 'right thing' when put to the test – without reflection or discussion but also without orders, and always chosing the most radical course of action possible.

The decisive element in this context turned out to be the fusion of the hitherto separate spheres of 'objectivity' and *Weltanschauung* among the leadership of the regime of terror: professionalism and qualif-ication, calculating expediency, the use of modern technology, a strict integration into the state administration on the one hand, and on the other hand a radical orientation – without personal emotion or motivation – towards an ideologically legitimized goal on the basis of a comprehensive doctrine and carried out by the elite of a National Socialist order.

The ideologue was also a specialist, the mass murderer an admin-istrative lawyer, the technocrat a fighter for his *Weltanschauung*. In the short as well as the long term this proved to be one of the decisive factors in the continuous radicalization and effectivity of the RSHA and the units and offices under its command.

In October 1943 Himmler told the leadership of SS and RSHA that the murder of the Jews was, and had to remain, an unwritten but honourable page in the book of history because the SS that had taken over this unpleasant but necessary task had nevertheless remained decent. His much-quoted Posen speech has to be seen in the context elaborated above and in this context only: the elite of the SS and, in particular, the leadership of the RSHA, composed of traditional office and of *Weltanschauungs*-corps, did what they did out of conviction and rejection of their moral tradition because they deemed it right and necessary, not because they were personally, emotionally, involved.

Werner Best – typically both the ideologue and lawyer of the Gestapo – once described this overcoming of traditional morale derived from *völkisch* laws (*völkische Lebensgesetze*), this execution of something inevitably necessary, though horrible, as 'a characteristic of morality' ('Merkmal der Sittlichkeit'). For further reading see Ulrich Herbert, *Best. Biographische Studien über Radikalismus, Weltanschauung und Vernunft, 1903–1989*, Bonn 1996; also for quotes and background literature. This chapter summarizes some of the finding from the project 'Weltanschauung und Diktatur', a collaboration with Michael Wildt, Karin Orth and Christoph Dieckmann between 1992 and 1995 in Hamburg. Karin Orth has written a collective biography of the leadership of concentration camps; Christoph Dieckmann works on a study of the politics of occupation and extermination in Lithuania, from 1941 to 1944. Michael Wildt will expand the questions raised in this chapter in a forthcoming work; for initial results of his research see Michael Wildt (ed.), *Die Judenpolitik des SD, 1935–1939*, Munich 1995.

HANS MOMMSEN

The Indian Summer and the Collapse of the Third Reich: The Last Act

The plethora of books and articles dealing with the history of the Third Reich and the Second World War tend to pay relatively little attention to the internal causes of the destruction of the Nazi regime, since it is obvious that Hitler's rule could not have been brought to an end by domestic opposition, but only by military force. The following analysis, however, argues that besides the military decay of the regime an accelerating process of internal dissolution accompanied its military setbacks and were without doubt related to them.

Setting aside this viewpoint, the historian is confronted with the question of why the Nazi dictatorship was able to face a period of continuous military defeats during the period from the summer 1944 to May 1945. There exist divergent opinions as to when the military situation finally became hopeless for the Nazi regime. One could even point to the battle before Moscow in December 1941 when the German armies lost their superiority in size versus the Red Army and had increasing difficulties replacing the huge amount of weaponry and military equipment they lost during the successful Soviet counteroffensive in the winter of 1941/2.[1]

Even if one admits that the German operations in 1942 might have tipped the balance again in favour of the Germans, the defeat and the surrender of the Sixth Army at Stalingrad on 31 January 1943 signified the ultimate turning point of the Second World War. This catastrophic event ultimately destroyed the myth of the invincibility of the German troops, after it had already been severely damaged by the defeat in North Africa and the lost air battle over the English

Channel. The regime reacted to this by desperate attempts to mobilize its hitherto insufficiently exploited manpower resources under the slogan of 'total war', a slogan coined by Joseph Goebbels in his notorious public speech in the Berlin sport palace on 18 February 1943, less than three weeks after the catastrophe of Stalingrad.[2]

Even if the Nazi leadership still clung to the illusion that a potential split between the Western Allies and the Soviet Union could save the Reich from imminent military defeat, from the summer of 1944 the strategic situation appeared to be hopeless. The Soviet breakthrough at the central sector of the Eastern front forced the German troops into a fundamentally defensive position against the overwhelming strength of the Red Army and did not allow them any chance of offensive operations.

Given these conditions, we need to ask why the regime apparently survived the sustained and accelerating military crisis until its ultimate demise in May 1945 and how the Nazi leadership still continued to mobilize remarkable defensive resources. Furthermore, in analysing this final phase of the European war we are given the impression that in its eclipse the true nature of the Nazi regime was exposed. This can be compared with the way in which people facing imminent death tend to return to the reminiscences and expectations of their youth, a phenomenon I try to describe by using the term 'Indian summer'. The period between July 1943, when Benito Mussolini was dismissed by Victor Emanuel with the backing of the Fascist Grand Council, and April 1945, when Hitler committed suicide, was on the one hand signified by never-ending military setbacks and on the other by an unremitting concentration of political power in the hands of the Nazi Party. During these last months of Nazi rule the party was able to complete its revolutionary agenda, which had been postponed immediately after the seizure of power in 1933/4.

From the outbreak of the war, there had been half-hearted attempts to increase the efficiency of the Reich administration, firstly with the instalment of Hermann Göring as the chief of the Reich Defence Council in 1939. But this failed to achieve the necessary integration of divergent departmental interests and to intensify the war production even after Fritz Todt and, his successor in 1941, Albert Speer, received plenipotentiary powers to run the armament industry.[3] But it was not until Stalingrad that Hitler's leading chieftains were prepared to accept the need to overcome the basic weaknesses of the leadership structure at the top of the Reich.

Goebbels's speech in the Berlin *Sportpalast* after Stalingrad demanded a readiness to accept 'total war', which meant the exploitation of under-used human resources, a drastic reduction in civilian consumption and the streamlining of the administration. However, attempts to regenerate the Reich Defence Council or to install a so-called three-man committee in order to enforce the overdue rationalization measures failed, partly because of the resistance of the Nazi Gauleiters who had successfully expanded their regional power and opposed any curtailment of their respective *Gau* economies.[4]

Despite Goebbels's exhortations, the lack of coordination within the Reich government persisted through the critical year of 1943. The fall of Mussolini threw its shadow on the domestic political scene in Germany and one reaction to it was the replacement of the Minister of the Interior, Wilhelm Frick, who for two years had pleaded to be relieved of his office, with Heinrich Himmler. Himmler seemed to guarantee that events similar to those that had happened in Italy would be effectively nipped in the bud.

Himmler, however, proved to be a rather weak chief of his ministry, being mostly dependent on his ministerial advisers, and he did not do much to stop the escalating administrative chaos as well as the infighting within party and state which absorbed the energies of the sub-leaders. Himmler remained involved with Gestapo and SD security measures, and failed to produce a programme of rationalization for the general administration.[5]

Not until the crisis of July 1944 did Goebbels's efforts to regenerate a rudimentary central government got the chance to find Hitler's approval, the latter being rather timid about any fundamental reform of the leadership structure. Goebbels and Bormann had long since realized that Hitler was somewhat of an obstacle to the implementation of the overdue mobilization of economic and manpower resources. Thus, he rejected almost all reform incentives presented by Goebbels or Bormann, believing they might create opposition amongst other sub-leaders or damage his own prestige. Therefore he did not give in to Goebbels's incessant pressure to dismiss Ribbentrop, the Minister of Foreign Affairs, who was held responsible for the desperate diplomatic isolation of the Reich, and the same was true with respect to the endeavours by Bormann and Himmler to dissuade Hitler from appointing Göring as his designated successor.[6] While Göring lost control of the air industry to Albert Speer, he preserved the prestige of still being second to Hitler within the Reich leadership.

Instead of seizing the reins of government, Hitler had to be carefully isolated from the changing opinions of external advisers and conflicting interests, to which he would respond by spontaneous decisions threatening any governmental continuity. In this state of indecision the decisive impetus for intensifying the German war effort was created by Albert Speer, Reich Minister for Munitions and War Production, who had succeeded in taking over almost all the prerogatives of the Four Year Plan office while preserving Göring's nominal status as its head.[7]

Moreover, relying on the unconditional support of the dictator, Speer was able to break the controlling power of the army and to replace the so-called *Heereswaffenamt* (armament office) with his ministry. In this way Speer became one of the most influential satraps within the regime, and significantly, the rumour sprang up that he might become the successor of the Führer, which immediately made Martin Bormann and Joseph Goebbels envious.[8]

It was symptomatic of the regime that, more important than the actual need to produce general reforms in order to strengthen the German war effort, was the alarming figure of Speer with his plenipotentiary powers over the economy that might supersede the influence of the party and might even surpass Goebbels in directly advising the dictator. Hitler himself neglected day-to-day politics more and more, and his energies were almost completely absorbed by his self-chosen supreme command over the military operations against the Soviet Union.

Speer was inclined to use unorthodox governmental methods and to circumvent ordinary administrative channels and legal procedures. Like the average Nazi leader, he preferred to rely on the personal loyalty of individuals rather than institutional patterns. In the short run this technique proved to be extremely successful and allowed him to multiply the armament output (although much of this was due either to the merit of his predecessor Fritz Todt or to manipulated statistics).[9] In the long run his system would have failed, but the military defeat obscured the consequences of the principle of *Menschenführung* (Personal Leadership).[10]

Confronted with the crises on the Eastern front, Speer presented an extended memorandum to Hitler, demanding the intensification of the armament efforts. Blaming the three-man committee for its obvious inefficiency, he pleaded for a strong leadership which should be dominated by personalities who were not involved in the infighting of the bureaucratic agencies and would not lose their nerve in crisis situations. This fell short of demanding a plenipotentiary for the realm of domestic politics.[11]

These ideas coincided with Goebbels's pressure for an internal dictatorship, and he did not hesitate to opt for an alliance with Speer, especially after similar attempts to win over Göring for any resolute action had failed completely. While Goebbels supported Speer's demands in a well-regarded article in the newspaper *Das Reich*,[12] the minister for Munitions and War Production presented a second memorandum in which he repeated his arguments for achieving a more efficient leadership and proposed Goebbels, whom he believed to be highly qualified, as the person with the ability to push this programme through the opposing interest groups.

Goebbels knew that the biggest obstacle to implementing his idea of an acting domestic dictatorship lay in Hitler's notorious distrust and fear for his own personal prestige. In his article in *Das Reich* Goebbels argued that the programme had found overwhelming approval amongst the German public, which may have been partly true, but was a skilfully designed move to overcome Hitler's apprehension.[13] Moreover, on 18 July he presented an analogous fifty-page memorandum to the Führer's Headquarters in which he reiterated his arguments of the *Sportpalast* speech of February 1943 and demanded the replacement of the three-man committee by an independent commissionership.[14]

The timing of Goebbels's initiative proved to be perfect. It necessarily strengthened his position in the summit conference that had been convened by Hitler for 22 July in order to discuss the Speer memorandum. At the meeting, Goebbels presented himself as the uniquely qualified candidate for the new commissionership and managed to get the endorsement of the leaders present, among them Bormann, Keitel, Speer, Funk and Lammers. Pointing at Hitler's usual hesitancy, he underlined the necessity of getting a unanimous vote for his nomination, and nobody dared to abstain.[15] Thus, on 25 July 1944 the Reich Minister for Propaganda and Popular Enlightenment, Joseph Goebbels, was entrusted by Hitler with the task of acting as the 'Reich Plenipotentiary for the Total War Effort'.

Hence, just five days after the abortive attempt of 20 July, Goebbels had gained a political position which just fell short of deputy to the Führer and which comprised according to his own words 'the domestic leadership'.[16] This, however, turned out to be more or less an illusion, because Goebbels had failed to obtain the authority to give orders either to the NSDAP or the army leadership, these being exempt from his overall authority to issue directives on the different administrative levels. Moreover, he overestimated his ability to overrule vested interests when implementing the mobilization of manpower, the closing down of those shops, factories and industries which did not serve the war effort, and the replacement of the ordinary public administration.

This was partly the consequence of Goebbels's perception of politics, which placed all emphasis on propagandistic methods, while underestimating the impact of bureaucratic procedures. He perceived his personal role as setting things in motion and functioning as a catalyst for the process of public mobilization. Symptomatic of this was his tendency to use the local and regional party institutions rather than the military apparatus and the ordinary administration to put through reform. Goebbels's unshakeable belief in the superiority of the principle of *Menschenführung* over public administration, which was typical for Nazi politics, only served to increase the notorious infighting between party and state.[17] The Propaganda Minister sought the support of the local and regional party organizations in order to implement his mobilization directives. In conjunction with this, he created mixed committees consisting of the functionaries on the *Gau* level, the regional administrative boards and affiliated party organizations which were meant to be in charge of the conscription for the army and the armament industries, but in fact turned out to be far less effective than the organization of the army district commands (*Wehrkreise*).[18]

Goebbels, however, did not expect that the immediate achievements of his mobilization campaign would make much impact on the almost desperate military situation, because it would take a couple of months until the recruitment of new soldiers and armament workers became effective. But he was convinced that the campaign was indispensable if his demand for 'total war' was not to lose its credibility. His belief in the impact of propagandistic indoctrination was revealed by his argument, that the 'total war' campaign would cause an 'incredible improvement in the public mood' and, thereby, lead to a galvanization of the people, who would 'gather fresh hope'.[19]

The propaganda about 'holding out' and 'seeing it through' could not be continued without also taking practical steps if it was to retain its credibility. The propaganda had, as Martin Broszat has argued with respect to the implementation of genocide, to be taken at its word.[20] Thus, it was primarily for propagandistic reasons that Goebbels advocated exhausting the last available human resources for the war effort, including the overdue obligatory work for women. He expected to achieve the total mobilization primarily by shifting the necessary competencies to the local and regional party organizations.

At the same time Martin Bormann, Chief of the Party Chancellery, came to similar conclusions and intensified his efforts to regenerate the numerically bloated but politically sterile party organization and to change it into a unified combat organization. Bormann found in this the support of Robert Ley, who, besides being the leader of the German Labour Front, was also a Reich Organization Leader of the NSDAP.[21] Both did their best to achieve the repoliticization of the party and its affiliated organizations and to restore the damaged public reputation of the movement which was known for an almost unimaginably high level of corruption and inertia.[22]

In order to achieve this, Bormann tried to activate the rank and file by continuously arranging obligatory membership assemblies, propaganda marches and public demonstrations. While the results were limited, the strategy nevertheless held the functionaries in line and regenerated intra-party communication. By the same token, Bormann tried to improve the party's contact with the population by introducing special office hours, so-called consultation evenings, where visitors could express their grievances. Significantly, these measures were based on the model of the Christian church. In conjunction with this, the local party organizations were ordered to arrange special obituary rituals in order to compete with the church funerals.[23]

More successful was Bormann's deliberate strategy to regain the political leadership for the party by taking over the care for those who had lost their homes on account of the Allied air offensive or had to leave the combat zones.[24] In conjunction with this, Bormann gave the order that the NSV, the National Socialist welfare organization, had to act expressly in the name of the political organization of the party.[25] By the same token, the party took over their authority for doing relief work from private relief organizations or the municipalities. This move proved to be quite effective. If one takes into account the fact that almost 80 per cent of the Germans in the Old Reich changed their place of residence due to war damage, air attacks or migration from the East and became dependent upon the support of the NSV, one can assess the socio-psychological impact of this strategy by which the party succeeded in partially restoring its public image.

Apart from the internal reactivation of the party and its attempts to present itself as the true representative of the *Volksgemeinschaft*, it continuously expanded its influence on the local and regional level by taking over public functions which hitherto had been performed by the traditional civil service. The growing interference of the party in the public sector was possible because of the plenipotentiary powers extended to the Gauleiters in their legal function as Reich Defence Commissioners, and in some cases even as chiefs of the civil administration.[26] In addition to this, there occurred a new wave of office patronage on the *Gau* and district level because many party dignitaries who had been sent to the East now tried to get positions in the public sector.

In order to describe the changing relationship between party and state Dietrich Orlow coined the term 'partification'. This means that the influence of the party on the lower levels of public administration expanded continuously, parallel to the growing influence of the local and regional Gestapo and SD, at the expense of the ordinary judiciary.[27] Symptomatic of this process was the fact that the Nazi Party became more and more involved as an auxiliary to the Security Police and the Gestapo. Later on the party became responsible for the fortification of defence lines as well as for sheltering the population which had to be expelled from the combat zones.[28]

In so far as the party was able to expand its political power and activity in this way it surpassed the wildest dreams the party leadership had entertained during the period of the seizure of power. This process, however, coincided with the slow decay of the political system under the impact of constant air attacks, increasing damage to the transport and communication systems, and the manpower shortage. Thus we are confronted with an antagonistic, and in a certain sense dialectic, process. On the one hand, the governmental system broke up, every initiative suffocated in endless quarrels between party and state agencies, communication between the ministries and the Führer Headquarters had shrunk to almost zero, the dictator was thoroughly isolated in his bunker below the Reich Chancellery and no longer appeared in the public.[29] On the other hand, this state of dissolution proved to be fertile ground for the party radicals who returned to their illusions of the so-called *Kampfzeit* and no longer met any resistance on the part of the conservative elite, which had been silenced by the events following the abortive coup of July 1944. Under these conditions, the party, presenting itself as capable of mobilizing 'the last strength', returned to the propagandistic self-perception of the time when it rose from a small splinter group to a virtual mass party. The military and political crisis which gripped the regime could no longer be denied, but it was blamed on the old conservative bureaucrats who lacked the necessary dynamic, strong will. Only the party and its 'spirit' could enforce an overall mobilization of the nation's strength and resources, while the sharing of political authority with the bourgeois notables was presented as the real cause of the Reich's military and political crisis. The foremost goal, therefore, had to consist in completing an homogeneous *Volksgemeinschaft*, not only racially, but also 'in spirit'.

Party propaganda spoke relentlessly of the crucial experience of the *Kampfzeit*, through which the obstacles could be overcome. The initial defeat of the movement on 9 November 1923 was taken as a proof that the party was invincible in the long run and that it depended upon the Powers of Will to overcome even the most difficult situations. A directive, issued by the Party Chancellery 29 September 1943, declared: 'The National socialist movement has mastered every situation. It has never allowed itself to be distracted by occasional setbacks or great difficulties',[30] and in materials designed as instructions for party speakers, one could read at the same time, that 'the struggle which we as the German people have to endure today is fundamentally the same struggle against the same enemy which the movement had to carry on at home in the years of the *Kampfzeit*.'[31] Not a single propaganda directive omitted reference to the *Kampfzeit* and its heroic idealization.

By these constant references to the party's glorious past the fiction was created that, if only the party took things in hand, victory would be imminent. This implied, however, that the compromises the party had made during the years of the seizure of power with the bourgeois elite had to be abolished and the National Socialist revolution, which then had been stopped halfway, should be completed by eliminating any non-National Socialist element in the public administration and society at large, either through the pressure of propaganda or by political coercion. Hence, the vision of unlimited party rule was inseparably connected with the extension of terror.

From the viewpoint of racial and political homogeneity as a precondition for the requested 'unity of the will' not only the destruction of the Jews and their complete deportation from the Reich, but also the cleansing of German society of former opponents or dissidents came to be of crucial importance. This completely a-historic and arbitrary position is difficult to understand, but it lay at the very foundation of the perception of politics by the Nazi leadership. In a way this position must be regarded as nostalgia for the Nazis' pseudo-idealist inheritance, but it was also influenced by Nietzschean philosophy, which culminated in the cult of the will and the notion that only through a decisionist break with the past could the vision of the 'Third Reich' be brought to reality.[32] This belief in the triumph of will had been typical of the early years of the movement, when only the vision of future victory could overcome bleak reality. During the regime phase this vision had become mixed with a pragmatic and cynical use of power, but now the party returned to its earlier position. A milestone on the road back to terrorist will-power was Goebbels's aforementioned speech in the Berlin *Sportpalast*, in which he announced that the promised victory would be achieved by a fanatical willpower to hold out to the last man and not by the availability of material resources, which appeared just as a means to attain this heroic purpose. The parallel incentive by Bormann and Ley to create an all-embracing ideological mobilization of the party fitted into this picture.[33]

The party's retreat into nostalgia for the *Kampfzeit* coincided with Hitler's personal conviction that the 'final victory' was the predestined outcome of the internal and external fight against the Jewish arch enemy, as his public utterances from 1943 onwards constantly show. In Hitler's mind the unity of the will was a pledge for final success, and one is reminded of the Hegelian assumptions of the relation between historical necessity and the true will of the acting politicians. In his last radio speech on 30 January 1945 Hitler argued that the 'internal unification' of the German people, which he attributed to himself and the Nazi movement and which he praised as a unique world historical achievement, was the basis of its invincibility.[34] It seems plausible that in this respect the influence of Nietzsche, possibly in a misinterpreted fashion, was at work.

Goebbels did not hesitate to support Hitler in his belief that the 'final victory' was just a question of willpower. He reminded his Führer of the crucial situation in December 1932 when Gregor Straßer had protested against the continuation of Hitler's 'policy of all or nothing' and predicted the breakdown of the party, while Hitler had decided in favour of preserving 'the purity of the National Socialist idea' against Straßer's readiness to sacrifice National Socialist principles and accept General von Schleicher's offer to enter a coalition government.[35] Goebbels also induced Hitler to use the model of Frederick the Great and his endurance in the Seven Years war. In this he supported Hitler in his belief that the 'purity of the will' must prevail in the long run. This was the main point of his last proclamation on 24 February 1945, the anniversary of the foundation of the NSDAP, where he evoked again 'our unshakeable will', which was to endure to the very end.[36] According to Hitler's vision the Allies would necessarily fail, not being capable of fighting a protracted war on German soil against the desperate resistance of the people who would defend every village, every house and every barn to the last man. Then the Western powers, at least, would have to acknowledge that it was futile to continue an increasingly costly battle between a whole people and an army of paid soldiers.[37]

Hitler's philosophy was disseminated by the propaganda which again became a major task of the party organization.[38] Therefore, the NSDAP returned to the ideological point of its departure and took refuge in the rhetoric that one had to start anew as well as in 'cult of the will' – the belief that sheer fanaticism and willpower could move mountains and save Germany from ultimate defeat. There emerged, however, an undercurrent of this propaganda which implied that in the unlikely case that immediate defeat could not be averted, the fight to the last man would at least secure 'the victory of the National Socialist idea' in a future Germany. Even in March 1943 Robert Ley tried to establish a 'Free Corps Hitler' – a typical harking back to the *Kampfzeit*, and even got approval from Hitler for that absurd enterprise.[39]

The 'hold-out' propaganda did not restrict itself to sheer rhetoric and terrorist intimidation against all who no longer put their confidence in the 'final victory', but had an effect in the military sector, too. A striking example can be seen in the decision to copy the model of the Political Officer in the Soviet Army, the political commissars, and to introduce 'National Socialist Leadership Officers'.[40] Selected and trained by the party organization, they would be attached to every military unit and guarantee the political liability of the commanders as well as enforcing the ideological indoctrination of the troops. The army had to agree to the conditions that the Leadership Officers should stay under the personal supervision of the Party Chancellery. Obviously Bormann calculated, that, in the event of demobilization, the party officers should replace the professionals and the nazification of the armed forces would, thereby, be automatically achieved.

The second aspect of this ideological offensive by the Party Chancellery was its plan to create a veritable people's army under the command of the party. The establishment of the *Deutscher Volkssturm*

(German Folkstormtroopers or Home Guard) in October 1944 was not only an attempt to mobilize the last levies after the ordinary troops had been decimated, but also a deliberate attempt to gain control over the army. After some quarrelling Bormann was given approval from the army leaders that the new militia would be led by party functionaries and under the supreme command of the Party Chancellery. Only the military equipment and the operational leadership lay in the hands of Heinrich Himmler, who was in command of the Reserve Army.[41]

This decision was evidently absurd, because the party was not in a position to provide militarily trained commanders, let alone to entrust the acting district and local party chiefs with this task, which consisted in the above-mentioned vision of the *Volksturm* defending their own villages. But for Bormann and Goebbels the military value of the militia was in fact of secondary importance. They viewed the function of the *Volksturm* essentially as a means of achieving the total ideological commitment of the whole people, which was, in their eyes, a pledge of final victory. Goebbels declared that the envisioned 'unified deployment of the entire people united in the idea of National Socialism' would lead to the formation of 'a holy people's army'.[42]

In the vision of Bormann and Goebbels the *Volksturm* presented the starting point for the intended amalgamation of the armed forces with the party, and his target was camouflaged with the usual propagandistic slogans. Goebbels returned to the last-fight discourse which we have already found to be typical of the late Hitler, when, while swearing in the *Volkssturm*, he publicly declared: 'We know that an idea lives, even if all its bearers have fallen. The enemy, who does not have more than he can deploy, will finally capitulate before the massed strength of a fanatically fighting people.'[43]

Here, as elsewhere, late Nazi propaganda borrowed heavily from Germany's national history. Thus it was no accident that the founding proclamation of the *Volkssturm* decreed by Heinrich Himmler was issued on 18 October 1944, the anniversary of the Battle of the Nations at Leipzig in 1813. In his speech Himmler referred expressly to the Prussian *Landsturm*, which had allegedly borne the main brunt of the battle, as a 'revolutionary people's movement'.[44] Total mobilization of the last energies of the people was regarded as the decisive factor which in the end would secure superiority to the German arms.

This mentality is reflected, too, in the well known UFA colour film *Kolberg* by Veit Harlan, whose production had been sponsored and heavily subsidized by Joseph Goebbels. Goebbels regarded it to be the equivalent of at least four military divisions.[45] The premiere was held in the fortress of La Rochelle on 30 January 1945 (the film reels were transported to the beleaguered city by plane and submarine), and it was subsequently shown for a couple of weeks in the Tauentzin Palace and some other Berlin cinemas. The film portrayed the allegedly heroic defence of the city of Kolberg against the superior forces of Napoleon I and the fiction that this fight was the origin of the German uprising in 1813.[46] It is difficult to believe that the film fulfilled its propagandistic function (anyhow, when Kolberg fell to Soviet troops on 18 March 1945, Goebbels made sure this event was ignored in the military situation report).[47]

The extent to which the mobilization campaign by Bormann, Ley and Goebbels convinced the party as well as the populace is difficult to assess. Their strategy culminated in forming a party task force which was to organize defence 'to the last man' in those communities which were already under attack, certainly to the anger of the military commanders in charge. In any case, the extreme pressure party functionaries as well as SS-troops exerted on the civilians prevented any effective resistance to the Nazis from emerging. By the same token, the 'hold-out' propaganda and the disciplinary measures taken against dissenting party functionaries explains why party leaders did not come up with initiatives of their own to stop the irresponsible fighting.

Conversely, the strong tensions between the party leaders prevented even the Gauleiters from attaining any common goals, unlike the leadership of the Italian Fascists in July 1943. Barely anyone dared to raise objections to the 'hold-out' propaganda, even after it became obvious that there was not the slightest military chance left. Symptomatic of this was the last encounter of the Gauleiters with the dictator on 25 February 1945 in the already heavily damaged building of the Reich Chancellery. There was only an obligatory handshaking. Bormann prohibited any exchange of opinions at that meeting under the pretext of not wanting to burden the Führer with details and once more vowed that the Gauleiters would 'stand and fall with the final victory'. The Führer myth was still alive.[48]

Moreover, the almost total influence of the Nazi Party had destroyed the last institutional backbones which could serve as a base for either resistance or dissent. A few days after the abortive plot of 20 July 1944 a British Intelligence report predicted that it would be futile to expect that there would be any central authority left 'exerting effective control over the country from which unconditional surrender could be accepted'.[49] In fact, since the failure of the attempt of 20 July, the military leadership definitely lost the ability to act on its own, especially after Hitler had filled the leading positions with Nazi fanatics.[50] The intensified party control of the armed forces was signified by permission for soldiers to retain their party membership while on duty and the introduction of the Hitler-salute into the army.

Moreover, since the summer of 1944 the leadership of the army lay exclusively in the hands of fanatical generals who welcomed unanimously the systematic ideological and racist indoctrination of the troops and did not hesitate to agree to the terrorist activity of the roving field court marshals and the military judiciary whose activities resulted in more than 30,000 executions.[51] Similarly, the almost omnipotent Gauleiters unleashed, in their function as Reich defence commissioners, an almost unrestricted wave of terror primarily upon the civil population, but also upon the many foreign forced labourers working in Germany. The Gauleiters presided over the drumhead courts which were formed by the ordinary judiciary in the respective commissioner districts and which brought death to thousands of innocent people. The regime did not hesitate to introduce liability of clan and kin (*Sippenhaft*) in cases where the intended defendants had escaped their grip.[52] Simultaneously, the Labor Education Camps established by the local and regional Gestapo in order to discipline the foreign and German workers in the armament industry became virtual death camps and were used for mass killings up to the last minutes of the war.[53]

It is open to further research as to how many Germans, Jews, Soviet POWs, forced labourers and other persecuted groups became victims of the death brigades of the SS, of the Gestapo and in many cases of self-created 'field marshals' during the last weeks of the regime's existence.[54] The background for the mass killings which started in the second half of 1944 and were continued until the ultimate breakdown of the Nazi government lay in the virtual identification of the 'internal' with the external enemy by Hitler and his chieftains. This deep-seated conviction implied the ruthless elimination of inimical elements or 'virtual' enemies of the regime. Therefore, the 'hold-out' strategy was inseparably bound up with the threat and practice of annihilation of potential dissidents. In addition, the desire to eliminate all those who might be potential obstacles to the restoration of the National Socialist idea explains phenomena like the so-called *Gitter-Aktion* of late 1944 in which several thousand former representatives of the Weimar Republic were imprisoned by the Gestapo with the possible intention of liquidating them as potential traitors to the German nation.[55] Thus the escalation of terror was directed against the German population as well, as far as it dared to resist to the 'hold-out' strategy.

At the same level was the Werwolf-propaganda which was promoted by Goebbels until the very end of the regime. A series of training camps which were attended by members of the Hitler Youth were systematically indoctrinating the youngsters to fight for the survival of the National Socialist idea even under the condition of Allied occupation. Not so much the guerrilla-function than the long-range ideological mission of the Werwolf characterized these late attempts to secure the commitment of future generations to National Socialism. The notorious overestimation of the impact of this ideology continued until the demise of the Nazi dictatorship.[56]

From this viewpoint it appears remarkable that the 'hold-out' propaganda began to transform itself into the strange expectation that the Nazi ideology would survive the breakdown of the regime and the death of the dictator and return in a renewed Germany. It is surprising that the Nazi leadership in its last moments was concerned primarily with organizing its historical afterlife and underwent a strange form of self-historicization.

These tendencies, interrelated with re-emerging nostalgia for the *Kampfzeit* which was bathed in an omnipresent heroic glow, stressed the purity and eternity of the Nazi vision. This reflects the fact that the Nazi elite finally looked back to the origins of the movement and its predominantly visionary concept of politics. At the bottom of all this lay the atrophy of the political system and German society, which was completely paralysed and unable to resist the suicidal course of the Nazi leadership, which itself was too deeply committed to the criminal deeds of the regime. This was part of the accelerating process of self-destruction which led to an increasing atomization of the governmental process and made the system incapable of ending a war which was evidently already lost. Symptomatic of this was the complete collapse of any authority in Germany after the fictitious unity of Hitler's personal rule disappeared. Neither the organizational stronghold nor its ideology survived the total collapse which accompanied the military defeat and the end of the war.

Notes

1. See *Das Deutsche Reich und der Zweite Weltkrieg*, published by Militär-geschichtliches Forschungsamt, vol 4: *Der Angriff auf die Sowjetunion*, Stuttgart 1983, 1023ff., 1085f.
2. Helmut Heiber (ed.), *Goebbels Reden 1932–1945*, Düsseldorf 1991, no. 17, pp. 172 ff.; cf. Günter Moltmann, 'Goebbels' Rede zum Totalen Krieg am 18. Februar 1943', *VfZ* 12 (1964) 13ff.; Willi A. Boelcke, 'Goebbels und die Kundgebung im Berliner Sportpalast vom 18. Februar 1943', *Jahrbuch für die Geschichte Mittel- und Ostdeutchlands* 19 (1970); Ludolf Herbst, *Der Totale Krieg und die Ordnung der Wirtschaft. Die Kriegswirtschaft im Spannungsfeld von Politik, Ideologie und Propaganda 1939–1945*, Stuttgart 1982, 198ff.
3. Cf. Dieter Rebentisch, *Führerstaat und Verwaltung im Zweiten Weltkrieg*, Frankfurt 1987, 121ff. and 132 ff.
4. Cf. Peter Longerich, *Hitlers Stellvertreter, Führung der Partei und Kontrolle des Staatsapparates durch den Stab Heß und die Partei-Kanzlei*, München 1992, 295; *Akten der Parteikanzulei*, Teil I, Mikrofiche No. 101 09595ff.
5. Cf. Dieter Rebentisch, *Führerstaat und Verwaltung im Zweiten Weltkrieg*, Stuttgart 1989, 499ff.
6. Cf. *Die Tagebücher von Joseph Goebbels* (=*Goebbels Tagebücher*), ed. Elke Fröhlich, München 1995, , T. II, vol. 15, pp. 296ff.; Ralph Georg Reuth, *Goebbels. Eine Biographie*, München 1990, 541.
7. S. Alfred Kube, *Pour le mérite und Hakenkeuz. Hermann Göring im Dritten Reich*, München 1986, 340f.
8. Cf. Gregor Jansen, *Das Ministerium Speer, Deutschlands Rüstung im Krieg*, Berlin 1968, 175f.; Hans-Joachim Weyres von Levetzow, *Die deutsche Rüstungswirtschaft von 1942 bis zum Ende des Krieges*, Ph.D. München 1975, 204.
9. See Richard J. Overy, *War and Economy in the Third Reich*, Oxford 1994, 356f.; cf. Janssen, *Das Ministerium Speer*, 175f.
10. S. Caplan, *Government without Administration. State and Civil Service in Weimar and Nazi Germany*, Oxford 1988, 336f.; cf. Rebentisch and Teppe, *Verwaltung contra Menschenführung*, 23ff.
11. Memorandum by Speer, 12 July and 20 July, 1944, printed in *Deutschlands Rüstung im Zweiten Weltkrieg. Hitlers Konferenzen mit Albert Speer*, ed. Willi A. Boelcke, Frankfurt 1969, No. 2; cf. Albert Speer, *Erinnerungen*, Frankfurt 1969, 405.
12. 'Führen wir einen totalen Krieg', *Das Reich*, 7 July 1944; Peter Longerich, 'Goebbels und der totale Krieg', *VfZ* 35 (1987), 298.
13. Cf. *Meldungen aus dem Reich, 1938–1945*, vol. 17, ed. Heinz Boberach, Hersching 1984, 6636ff.
14. Printed in Longerich, 'Joseph Goebbels und der totale Krieg', 305–14.
15. Chefbesprechung on 22 July 1944 (BA Potsdam R 43II/664a, p. 87).

16. Cf. *Goebbels Tagebücher* II, vol. 11, 27 February 1943, where he considered the plan to replace the three-man committee by the Reich Ministerial Council for Defence with himself as a deputy.

17. See the decree related to the total war effort of 16 Aug. 1944 in BA Potsdam R 18/1278, folios 35–7.

18. See Horst Matzerath, *Nationalsozialismus und kommunale Selbstverwaltung*, Stuttgart 1970, 240f.; Rebentisch, *Falirerslogt und Veroal fung* 526f. and letter from Stuckart to Bormann, 19 Dec. 1944 (BA Koblenz, R 18/1263, fol. 19).

19. Longerich, 'Goebbels und der totale Krieg', 313; cf. chief meeting on 22 July 1944: 'Die Reform des öffentlichen Lebens werde zum Teil nur optischen Charakter haben können, doch dürfe die Bedeutung solcher Maßnahmen nicht unterschätzt werden' (fol. 86). (The reform of public life will partly have a cosmetic character, but the significance of such measures ought not to be underestimated.)

20. Martin Broszat, 'Führerbindung und soziale Motivation des Nationalsozialismus', in: Broszat, *Nach Hitler. Der schwierige Umgang mit unserer Geschichte*, München 1988, 32f.

21. Cf. Ronald Smelser, *Robert Ley, Hitler's Labor Front Leader*, Oxford 1988, 284f, 290f.

22. See the forthcoming Bochum Ph.D. dissertation by Armin Nolzen on *Martin Bormann and the Restructuration of the NSDAP 1941–45*.

23. *Verfügungen, Anordnungen, Bekanntgaben*, ed. Partei-Kanzlei der NSDAP, 7 vols, München 1942–5, here vol. 4 (1943), pp. 24ff.; vol. 5 (1944), A5/43, 17 Febr. 1943; 'Gedankengänge zu den Generalmitgliederappellen', 1943 (BA Potsdam NS6/408, fol. 397–404); Akten der Partei-Kanzlei T. II, nos 06561ff.

24. Cf. Martin Rüther, *Köln, 31. Mai 1942: Der 1000-Bomber-Angriff* (Kölner Schriften zur Geschichte und Kultur 18), Köln 1992, 66f.

25. Cf. Herwart Vorländer, *Die NSV. Darstellung und Dokumentation einer nationalsozialistischen Organisation*, Boppard 1988, document no. 293, p. 514; cf. pp. 173f.

26. Cf. Karl Teppe, 'Der Reichsverteidigungskommissar. Organisation und Praxis in Westfalen', in Rebentisch and Teppe (eds), *Verwaltung contra Menschenführung*, 279 and 299ff.

27. Dietrich Orlow, *The History of the Nazi Party*, vol. II: *1933–1945*, Pittsburgh 1973, esp. 345ff.

28. See Peter Hüttenberger, *Die Gauleiter*, Stuttgart 1969, 189; RMdI to Himmler, on 9 Sept. 1944, concerning preparation for the defence of the Reich territory, in *Ursachen und Folgen*, vol. 21, pp. 555f. and the decree by Hitler on 1 Sept. 1944, in *Akten der Partei-Kanzlei*, no. 10201359ff.

29. See Trevor-Roper, *The Last Days of Hitler*, London 1958, pp. 58ff.

30. *Verfügungen, Anordnungen, Bekanntgaben*, A 55/1943 on 29 Sept. 1943, vol. 4, p. 9.

31. Aufklärungs- und Rednermaterial der Reichspropagandaleitung der NSDAP, Lieferung 9 (Sept. 1943), pp. 2 and 4.
32. See J. Peter Stern, *The Fuehrer and the People*, London 1975.
33. See Meldungen zur Versammlungswelle der NSDAP, 8 Nov. 1943 (BA Potsdam NS 6/408, fol. 397, 404; see also action platform by the Reichspropagandaleitung on 3 July 1943 (Akten der Partei-Kanzlei, T. II, No. 06561ff.).
34. In *Ursachen und Folgen*, vol. XXII, pp. 480ff.
35. See *Goebbels Tagebücher*, T. II, vol. 15, pp. 232f.; cf. vol. 7, 23 Jan. 1943, pp. 177f.; see also Udo Kissenkoetter, *Gregor Straßer und die NSDAP*, Stuttgart 1978, pp. 202f. Straßer's resignation from his party offices occurred in an almost hopeless situation.
36. *Ursachen und Folgen*, 484ff.
37. Cf. Hitler's proclamation to the New Year, on 1 Jan. 1945 (*Ursachen und Folgen*, vol. XXII, p. 325).
38. See Anlage zum Rundschreiben 255/1944 of 21 Sept. 1944 (Anordnungen etc. 1944, 80180634f.): "Der Führer hat befohlen: . . . Jeder Bunker, jeder Häuserblock in einer deutschen Stadt und jedes deutsche Dorf muß zu einer Festung werden, an der sich der Feind entweder verblutet oder die ihre Besatzung im Kampf Mann gegen Mann unter sich begräbt." (The Führer has ordered: . . . every dugout, every housing block in a German town and every village must become a fortress against which the enemy either bleeds to death or whose defenders bury themselves in the hand-to-hand struggle).
39. See *Goebbels Tagebücher*, T. II, vol. 15, pp. 637f. and 646f.
40. See Volker Berghahn, 'NSDAP und 'Geistige Führung' der Wehrmacht 1939–1945', *VfZ* 17 (1969), 17–71; Arne W. G. Zoepf, *Wehrmacht zwischen Tradition und Ideologie. Der NS-Führungsoffizier im Zweiten Weltkrieg*, Frankfurt 1988.
41. See Franz W. Seidler, *Deutscher Volkssturm. Das letzte Aufgebot, 1944/45*, München 1989, 383ff.
42. Gauleiter meeting on 8 Aug. 1944 Wolfgang Bleyer, 'Pläne der faschistischen Führung zum totalen Krieg', *ZfG* 17 (1969), 132f.
43. *Zeitschriftendienst/Deutscher Wochendienst*, ed. Reichsministerium für Volksaufklärung und Propaganda, Berlin, ZD 285. Cf. 154th edn of 20 Oct. 1944: 'Wir wissen, daß eine Idee lebt, auch wenn ihre Träger gefallen sind'. (We know that an idea lives even if its bearers have fallen.)
44. Seidler, *Deutscher Volkssturm*, 383.
45. S. Veit Harlan, *Im Schatten meiner Filme. Selbstbiographie*, Gütersloh 1966.
46. Cf. '*Kolberg*' – Ein Film, Ein Beispiel, *Völkischer Beobachter*, 31 Jan. 1945, and François Courtage and Pierre Cadars, *Geschichte des Films im Dritten Reich*, München 1975, 217ff. and Erwin Leiser, *Deutschland erwache. Propaganda im Film des Dritten Reiches*, 3rd. edn, Hamburg 1989, 111f.
47. *Goebbels Tagebücher*, T. II, vol. 15, p. 542.

48. Rudolf Jordan, *Erlebt und erlitten. Der Weg eines Gauleiters von München nach Moskau*, Freiburg 1971, 252ff.; Karl Wahl, '. . . *es ist das deutsche Herz*'. *Erlebnisse und Erkenntnisse eines ehemaligen Gauleiters*, Augsburg 1954, 385f.
49. Records of the JCS, Part I, 1942–45, European Theater, Reel 10; German translation in Rolf-Dieter Müller and Gerd R. Ueberschär, *Kriegsende 1945. Die Zerstörung des Deutschen Reiches*, Frankfurt 1994, 41.
50. Partei-Kanzlei Bekanntgabe 208/44, 30 Aug. 1944 (Verordnungen etc., vol. VIII, pp. 8f.); cf. Orlow, *History of the Nazi Party*, vol. II, p. 465.
51. Manfred Messerschmitt and Fritz Wüller, *Die Wehrmachtsjustiz im Dienste des Nationalsozialismus. Zerstörung einer Legende*, Baden-Baden, 1987; cf. Jürgen Thomas, 'Die Wehrmachtsjustiz im Zweiten Weltkrieg', in Norbert Haase and Gerhard Paul (eds), *Die anderen Soldaten*, Frankfurt 1995, 43.
52. Cf. Klaus-Dieter Henke, *Die amerikanische Besetzung Deutschlands*, München 1995, 845ff.; Ralph Angermund, *Deutsche Richterschaft 1919–1945*, Frankfurt am Main 1990, 215ff.
53. Gabriele Lotfi, *KZ der Gestapo. Arbeitserziehungslager im Dritten Reich*, München 2000, 292ff.
54. Klaus-Dietmar Henke, *Die amerikanische Besetzung Deutschlands* (Quellen und Darstellungen zur Zeitgeschichte 27), München 1995, 845ff.; Angermund, *Deutsche Richterschaft 1919–1945*, pp. 215f.
55. See Martin-Broszat and Elke Froehlich et al. (eds), *Bayern in der NS-Zeit*, vol. IV, Munich 1981, 660ff.
56. *Goebbels Tagebücher*, T. II, vol. 15, pp. 393f., 457, 498; see Charles Whiting, *Werewolf. The Story of the Nazi Resistance 1944–1945*, London 1972, pp. 145f. and Arno Rose, *Werwolf 1944–1945*, Stuttgart 1980, pp. 70ff.; Henke, *Amerikanische Besetzung*, pp. 948ff. Goebbels expected that about 10 per cent of the German population could be activated by the Werwolf, *Goebbels Tagebücher*, vol. 15, p. 673.